Praise for
The Art of Doubling Down

Everyone fails. The problem is that not everyone rises from the ashes once they have failed. Most people choose to become a victim and wrap themselves in their failure to the point that it becomes their identity. *The Art of Doubling Down* can help you break the victim cycle. Anthony Russo does a powerful job of walking you through the steps to rising up from your failure. He has lived it, just like we all have, but the difference is he knows the way back and the path to success. This is a book you will come to highly value on the journey of life.

-**Chad Prather,** host, Blaze TV's *The Chad Prather Show*

If you've ever been knocked down by failure and thought it was the end, *The Art of Doubling Down* by Anthony Michael Russo will show you how failure can be your greatest ally. Through gripping stories and personal experiences, Russo proves that failure is not the end, but a powerful stepping stone towards success and happiness. Get ready to transform your perspective and embrace failure as the fuel that propels you to new heights in life and business. Play to win by mastering the art of doubling down on YOU!

-**Mike Fallat,** owner of Dreamstarters Publishing

In *The Art of Doubling Down,* Anthony Russo provides stories, inspiration, and actionable steps to turn perceived failures into powerful fuel for success.

-**Ian Altman**, best-selling author of *Same Side Selling*

The Art of Doubling Down by Anthony Russo is a powerful and thought-provoking book that challenges our perception of failure and redefines it as a steppingstone to success. Russo takes readers on a journey of self-discovery and growth, urging them to hit their mental Big Red Button and initiate a holy shift in their thinking. *The Art of Doubling Down* is not a book that offers quick fixes or empty promises. It is a call to action, a guide to reshaping our mindset and embracing failure as an integral part of the journey to success. Russo's insights and practical advice will empower readers to overcome their fear of failure, redefine their relationship with risk, and navigate the challenges that come their way with resilience and determination. Russo empowers readers to step out of their comfort zones, embrace vulnerability, and unleash their true potential. I highly recommend *The Art of Doubling Down* to anyone seeking personal and professional growth. Russo inspires readers to embark on a transformative journey toward a life filled with success, fulfillment, and the confidence to double down on their dreams.

-**Eric Konovalov,** published author, business coach, and founder of Relentless Goal Achievers

The Art of Doubling Down

The Art of Doubling Down is not just a book; it's a life-changing manual for those who are ready to rewrite their stories! It's a compelling masterpiece that takes you on an extraordinary journey through the untold power of failure and how it can become the catalyst for unparalleled success. But Anthony's book is not *just* a call to embrace failure; it's an invitation to embrace the true essence of life, where growth and achievement are born from resilience and determination. Whether you're an entrepreneur, an artist, a student, or simply an individual yearning to achieve greatness, *The Art of Doubling Down* will serve as a guiding light, reminding you that failure is not the end but a stepping stone on the path to success.

-**Maggi Thorne,** seven-time American Ninja Warrior, CEO
of JoyFlowCo, empowerment advocate

Anthony Russo has crafted an absolute gem that will captivate and empower all those seeking to redefine failure. Through his profound insights, readers are driven to transform their own failures into triumphant victories. This is an absolute must-read for anyone on the journey of personal growth and self-empowerment.

-**Dave Brown,** serial entrepreneur

UNLOCK THE SECRET TO HOW
FAILURE ACCELERATES YOUR SUCCESS

The Art of
DOUBLING
DOWN

ANTHONY MICHAEL RUSSO

NEW YORK

LONDON • NASHVILLE • MELBOURNE • VANCOUVER

The Art of Doubling Down

Unlock the Secret to How Failure Accelerates Your Success

Published in New York, New York, by Morgan James Publishing. Morgan James is a trademark of Morgan James, LLC. www.MorganJamesPublishing.com

Proudly distributed by Publishers Group West®

Morgan James BOGO™

A **FREE** ebook edition is available for you or a friend with the purchase of this print book.

CLEARLY SIGN YOUR NAME ABOVE

Instructions to claim your free ebook edition:
1. Visit MorganJamesBOGO.com
2. Sign your name CLEARLY in the space above
3. Complete the form and submit a photo of this entire page
4. You or your friend can download the ebook to your preferred device

ISBN 9781636982588 paperback
ISBN 9781636982595 ebook
Library of Congress Control Number: 2023940724

Cover & Interior Design by:
Christopher Kirk
www.GFSstudio.com

Morgan James is a proud partner of Habitat for Humanity Peninsula and Greater Williamsburg. Partners in building since 2006.

Get involved today! Visit: www.morgan-james-publishing.com/giving-back

To Pops,
As time goes by since you passed, I appreciate your impact on my life more and more. You weren't perfect by any means, but it turns out, some of your greatest flaws and failures turned into the gifts and lessons that became this book.

Table of Contents

Preface xiii
Introduction: The Holy Shift—The Big Red Button 1

Chapter 1 | Redefining Failure 5
Chapter 2 | Discovering How to Double Down 19
Chapter 3 | The Double Down Lifestyle 31
Chapter 4 | Flipping Losses into Wins 45
Chapter 5 | Explaining Micro & Macro Failures 59
Chapter 6 | Overriding Failure 101 75
Chapter 7 | Overriding Failure Through Inspiration 87
Chapter 8 | Overriding the Unknown 103
Chapter 9 | Mental Fortitude—The Ultimate
           Mental Override 117
Chapter 10 | Course Correct—The Ultimate Set-Up 135
Chapter 10.2 | Double Down or Bust 145

Acknowledgments 149
About the Author 151

Preface

I hope what you read in this book inspires you, makes you think, motivates you, and causes you to take action in your own life and create the change you need to be the best version of you. David Goggins, an ultra-marathoner, author, and inspirational public speaker, talks about the two kinds of people that read books like this, theorists and practitioners.

The theorist is simply someone who accumulates information, always learning, always reading. A practitioner is someone who jumps in and makes it happen. They will put themselves through pain and misery to put in the work that theorists will only read about. Theorists are talkers, practitioners are not only doers who lead by example, but can also talk about what they've accomplished. David is a perfect example of the quintessential practitioner.

The core concept in this book is the ***power of failure.*** It's not going to be all warm and fuzzy, there will be some points that make you uncomfortable and challenge your beliefs in the meaning of progress and perfection. It may even go against the grain of how you were raised and what you've been told for decades. Please know the discomfort that this book may put you through is intentional. Because life is not perfect, we all have difficult times, but the happiness of the good times is a direct result of how we handle the failures that happen to us along the way.

I'm going to challenge you right off the bat with a superhero movie anecdote. I use a superhero reference because . . . well . . . it fits here, and second because far too often we look to other people to save us from bad circumstances. We look to loved ones, friends, the government and so many other random places when we all have the power to be our own superhero. If you wait for someone to be your superhero, you're destined for disappointment.

In time you will know what it is like to lose, to feel so
desperate that you're right, yet to fail nonetheless,
dread it, run from it, destiny (failure) still arrives.
(Thanos, from *Avengers Infinity War*)

Superheroes are accustomed to winning, and in Avengers Infinity War, all of them, from Captain America and Iron Man to Spiderman, get their butts handed to them. This was jarring for the audience. They waited an entire year and forked out $1.2 billion worldwide, just during the sequel's opening weekend, to find out how these superheroes would overcome their circumstances. The answer for them is the same as it is for us when we fail. To double down and fight back from failure.

I grew up in a household where every penny mattered. My mother was in college and my father was a handicapped, compulsive gambler. Most people would just look at the tragedy, the unpredictability, or pain of it all; however, I was able to gain something from the experience. While my father's gambling was reckless, he inadvertently taught me a principle that powered me through life and has helped me build successful businesses and a fulfilling life. His lesson? Never give up no matter the cost; eventually, life will return you the favor. A much better practice in life than in gambling.

I had learned the art of selling and later started my own business. Even though I accumulated large profits, I was challenged with many obstacles along the way. The pressures of keeping my business thriving while undergoing uncalculated risk put me on the search to handle difficulties better. After one night in the casino, it dawned on me that if I applied the same methods used in betting, my business mindset would be unstoppable. Light bulbs kept appearing in my brain, forcing me to do research and try this method out. I can confidently say, "It works!" I was able to build a seven-figure business in eighteen months by never giving up and doubling my bet. I want to show you how you can use these techniques to develop the mental tenacity to "override" every obstacle and turn defeats into playbooks for success.

Anthony Russo

Introduction

Holy Shift—The Big Red Button

O ver the course of this book, I am going to encourage you to hit your mental Big Red Button. We must begin telling our brain, Holy Sh*t (or Shift,) we need to completely change and unlearn our thought process on failure. This is going to be a huge shift and it won't come easy, but it is going to be worth it.

The big red button, aka the Deadman's Switch, aka the kill switch, are a few of the common names that describe override systems. Even though each of them has a slightly different definition, they all perform one basic function; to take over and prevent harm when the user is incapacitated or unable to use the machine or device properly.

For example, the "kill switch" as its name suggests, is a device intended to stop a machine (or activate one) if the human operator is unable to and is a form of fail-safe. They are commonly used in industrial applications like trains, cranes, lawn mowers, jet skis, and more... The switch in many of these cases is held by the user and turns off if they let go.

Hold on to that thinking and consider this. One of the most intricate and elaborate "machines" that was ever created was the human mind. According to an article in *The Scientific American,* the human brain weighs about three pounds and is comprised of the cerebrum, the largest portion of the brain that performs all higher cognitive functions and the cerebellum, which is responsible for motor functions, coordination, movement and balance. There are approximately *one hundred billion neurons* that run information to and from your brain for everything we see, think, or do. These neurons move information at different speeds, depending on their particular function. Why is this significant here?

It proves that even though the brain is one of the smallest parts of the human body, it is also the most intricate, complicated and amazing. Our brain is the ultimate "override" button. Throughout this book we will learn to build a new muscle in our brain that allows us to better control the big red button and take control of our "kill switch." Only then can we begin to reverse the crippling effects of failure and rewire the memories of those failures to help set us up for future success.

The key elements are going to be to change the perception of failure. This is that "Holy Shift." I can relate to every great failure story, whether it be Thomas Edison's 10,000 ways a light bulb doesn't work, Walt Disney failing time and again, or even Oprah getting fired from TV jobs. I understand how one can get discouraged and caught up in the losses of life, and how, in this age of social media, disappointment is put into hyperdrive.

All we see when we open our phones is people sharing photos of all their best moments on Instagram, Facebook, Twitter, Tik Tok…whatever. In recent years that has been split with politics, but the "perfect image," is still prevalent. It has forced us into a short-term focus on unattainable goals without a view of the big picture. It's also a vicious cycle. I can tell you the people posting their perfect vacation are looking at other people's business triumphs the week they get home wondering why that isn't them in that moment. We are always looking at someone else's lawn and wondering why ours doesn't look the same.

Every success story has a deep seated relationship to the failures that went into it. Whether it's a failure of a business, an idea, a relationship or a personal goal, we tend to stay stagnant in the sadness and recovery phase. I have proven that the distance between failure and success isn't as far away as most may think.

They can be compared to a long-distance relationship. The saying is "Distance makes the heart grow fonder." In other words, failure can get you closer and more passionate about success. In this book, I will share methods on how doubling down and negative progression enabled me to successfully build a million-dollar company in less than two years. This concept didn't come from a place of success either, it came from a father's addiction, and the pain of a child that, when used for good, is integral each day of my life to how I learned to face adversity and plan for my future.

Chapter 1

Redefining Failure

M y goal for you in reading this book is to make you so strong mentally that you will be able to attack your future without question or doubt, so that no matter what happens you will be successful in your direction and your drive. The fact is, we've become so afraid of failure that we make it impossible to succeed. You are going to be so mentally tough by the time you put this book down and close the back cover that you will be different. I hope I will change you. Whatever goals you have in front of you will no longer feel like an obstacle, but just part of your journey. How does this start? It starts with completely unlearning how you feel about failure and risk and redefining it.

First, I want to be clear, I have failed more times than I have succeeded, but I always got back off the canvas, I always got off the mat, I always pulled myself off the floor and you know what's crazy? It always worked out (even when it seemed as if it hadn't.)

This first step that I will challenge you with is the most difficult. This is where you step up to the table. Getting started, taking the first step and changing the previous way you have done things your whole life. Changing mindset is a daunting task. Change is one of the hardest human actions because it requires you to look inside yourself and completely turn your very comfortable and set beliefs into something much rawer. This takes something known as vulnerability and flexibility and it's HARD. I want to be very clear, this journey I am going to take you on will not be easy, but I promise you it will be worth it. Les Brown has a great quote where he says,

If you do what is easy, life will be hard,
but if you do what is hard, life will be easy.

LET'S GET TO WORK

Most people are at a stalemate, stuck, and looking for answers. If this is you, just use that as a sign that you are ready, ready to make a change. Everyone is at a different stage in their march towards success and happiness. Maybe you are close, and all you need is a nudge to keep pushing and avoid being the average person that is content with "better than okay but less than great." You'll see that I use some gambling references in this book, and I'll get more into that philosophy a little and why it's a theme.

In Blackjack, it's always suggested to do the same thing whenever you have a 16 against a face card. I always hit here, because I never want to think, "well what if," and technically the odds are in my favor, but only if I stay consistent. Key word, consistent. So, when you've been pushing harder and harder to succeed, know that there will be a point when something will go wrong, and you'll want to quit. It's a common philosophy that the closer one gets to a breakthrough, the harder things will get. There will almost always be a huge challenge right before breaking through that barrier. Whether you are at the beginning of this massive shift in your life or looking to breakthrough, understand that challenges are always knocking at your door.

For us to redefine failure, we need to start by defining risk. Risk is a trigger word for some and causes an undue fear based on prior failures. So, let's start by defining risk.

By definition, risk means a situation involving exposure to danger.

Risk is based on taking a chance on an outcome that could lead to failure and disappointment. We've been programmed to be afraid of physical risk, emotional risk, and that jumping in is associated with almost certain pain. Let's change that thought process and realize that a life without risk is a life without reward. Living in your comfort zone is a life full of fear. If you lived a whole life this way, you wouldn't have graduated from crawling to walking. You'd be still crawling all over the world. Even though we, as toddlers, aren't fans of falling, we get past it, and we try over and over again until we start to walk, and we fall until we get better at it.

Then over time, years, milestones and more, we start to have an unrealistic fear of falling and of failing in general. So again, what is risk? Risk is something that feels uncontrolled, and a fear of losing something of perceived value.

Like it or not, life is full of risks, and the more you want to achieve the more you are going to have to take risks. If you look at life from a gambling perspective, you can't make what you don't put on the table. So, if you want to play it safe and keep what you have and never improve or grow and change… stay away from the table of life, because the journey to success and fulfillment is going to require navigating risk.

We have been trained to avoid fear. Let's consider how our childhoods mold our concept of risk. Depending on our age and generation, we all have a slightly different but similar way we learned about risk. The prevailing way people were taught to parent was to feel as though they were to protect their children from risk. It's not a bad thought, but it subconsciously puts a huge fear of risk in us for the rest of our lives. Let's break that.

A very common truism in life, from investing to day-to-day self-reflection is, *"You can't make what you don't put on the table."* If you're not willing to play, life isn't going to pay. You simply aren't giving yourself an opportunity to win.

In the world of investing, if you don't put money into the stock market or in business investments, you will be forever destined to never make more than your yearly salary. Exponential growth is a mathematical concept that shows how small percentages of growth, year after year, can set you up for a prosperous and full life. What's interesting to people that don't fully understand investing, especially when it comes to mutual funds or life insurance policies, is that there is no such thing as a straight line of positive results. (To be clear there are hundreds of kinds of investing, and this kind of investing is just a portion of a balanced portfolio, so I don't want anyone to think I'm saying Mutual funds are the way to go. It's just for the purposes of this illustration.)

Typically, money is deposited on a regular basis and, if you watch your investment account, you'll drive yourself crazy because it will ebb and flow with the market. Sometimes you'll be losing, and you'll see your net worth in the mutual fund go down and down, but meanwhile you are still investing as values go down. Technically, you are able to double up on what you own at a lower cost and, in the end, as the ebbs and flows change their value this consistency and willingness to keep putting an investments in there, (even when it seems like you are losing and not wanting to continue to risk) always, based on the last 100 years of the stock market, has a positive pay off.

So, what does this all mean? If you aren't investing in risk, then you have no chance to excel, and will continue to flatline. Notice even the human heartbeat goes up and down constantly throughout the day. It's bound to happen and, if you really think about it, we are meant to have ups and downs, hell, our heart is even built this way. Even if you aren't an investor in the stock market or other options, you can still look at risk in terms of the chances you take in your job, or in your life. If you don't take a risk and put yourself out there, you aren't giving yourself the opportunity to get promotions, excel, or have a successful business. Yes, you might not feel as many of the low lows, but that just means you'll have that many less lessons to grow from.

There is not a single business that became successful without a decent amount of risk.

So, as humans we fear risk, but why? Were we born this way? Is this human nature? NO. When we are born, we start with two fears – fear of loud noises and fear of falling. From there we begin to develop fears due to environment and experience. Then various life experiences and faulty messaging causes our fears. Some of these fears are rational and some are irrational.

Rational fear is a reaction to a real threat where we must protect ourselves. Irrational fear is something we fear, even though there is no direct threat to us. Rational fear is something that we are consciously aware of. It comes from the human brain and is brought about by genetics. This fear is a reaction to a real threat where we feel as though we have to protect ourselves. Rational fears are something very tangible like pain, height, darkness, etc. You know what these fears are, you know what you have to do to face them and can actively change your brain to overcome them.

Irrational fear is a reaction to a person or event, even though there is no direct threat to us but has developed from a traumatic experience. It causes us to avoid situations pertaining to that fear. These are things like fear of commitment because people have been hurt in the past, and, of course, FEAR OF FAILURE, because of the feeling they have had in the past when they have failed or more importantly the stigma, we as a society have put on failure.

Experts agree that the more we begin to understand about those experiences that caused the fear, the easier it is to get past them. Hopefully, reading this book will start to shift your mindset, so you can see that the fear of failure is an irrational fear, and we'll change that fear in a fire, a fire to burn through all your obstacles on your roadmap to success and becoming a better version of yourself. Failure is a necessary tool that lights the fire and paves the path.

The way past our fear of risk-taking is to understand the origin of this deep-rooted fear. We fear risk-taking because we tend to equate risk with loss instead of reward.

Our terminology itself tends to instill fear in the action. We have phrases such as, "Don't risk it," or "It's not worth the risk." This makes it seem as though risk is going to put us in an adverse position. The problem behind this is that we place risk in the category of, "only use if it's almost certain it will net a reward." Unfortunately, that mindset keeps us too reserved as a people, and we disassociate the concept that often the reward is the lesson learned from taking that risk and failing.

Risk can be deemed synonymous with the concept of stepping up to the "table," aka this game we call life. It is true that you can't lose what you don't "bet," but likewise you also can't win anything of consequence either. Here I'll make a poker analogy. Eventually you have to take a risk and make a bet that still faces certain loss. Why? Because losing a hand allows you to learn something about the people you are playing against. You'll often hear Texas Hold'em players say, "I'll pay to see them." That means they have the feeling they are going to lose the hand, but they have hung in long enough with enough money already bet on the table, that they want to learn something about the player they are playing against. So even in a loss where they have risked a sizeable portion of their chips, they can learn better how their opponent plays, bets, bluffs, etc. Essentially learning information to use in the future despite losing that singular hand.

Now that we have the irrational fear of risk and failure outlined, let's start dismantling the ideology around it. No better example than the GOAT himself, Michael Jordan. He once said, "Whenever I was working out and got tired and figured I ought to stop, I'd close my eyes and see that list in the locker room without my name on it, and that usually got me going again."

What was MJ referring to? It's the story of him being cut from his varsity high school team as a sophomore. No matter if you've heard the story or not, and I assume most of you have… it never gets old. At the time, the varsity team had too much seniority and they needed size over talent, so they took Jordan's friend as the only sophomore because he was six feet, six, and Jordan was still only five feet, ten. This was a much better situation for Jordan, but, as we all know, it doesn't seem that way in the moment. The rejection and failure of not making the team crushes people, and in some cases, people can't come back from it. However, Jordan used this failure as fuel and as an experience to learn from. By being on JV he got much more playing time, and instead of being a substitute throughout the season he got to be a starter. On top of that, because he felt passed over, he practiced, trained, and played with a chip on his shoulder from that moment until the end of his career.

Here is the trick, we must re-define failure in our brains from perceiving it as a roadblock, and instead, switching it to a steppingstone. The first thing that gets people bogged down on failure is the belief that we should be great right away and on the first try. It's common for us to think this way because we are such a result-based society. However, results take time, daily practice and extreme focus.

It's important to understand that we typically start out from a place of mediocrity and often, complete failure. Even when someone is "a natural" at something, that just means they have a basic ability to learn quickly, and the passion to have that ability honed into something great. It all starts with the with that first step, followed by practice, consistency, and, yes, failures along the way. I like to relate this to snowboarding, that I took up in my early thirties. (Yes, I know that's odd.) When I began with this hobby, I really sucked for the first year...and hell, even well into the second. I was up, then down, up down, fall, get up, hot tub, ice, pain, what am I doing?

Now things are completely different. I cruise, listen to music and feel one with the world around me. I only get sore if I take a bad spill, and I'm in entering my forties! This was just my personal experience. I enjoy snowboarding and, over time, have improved like anyone could that keeps trying and keeps risking failure. A great example is the winter Olympics. I suggest watching the half pipe where they do 720s, 900s, and big airs like it's a walk in the park.

I want you to think for a second. Did these athletes strap into a snowboard when they were four years old and *boom*, they were able to do flips and tricks . . . no. Their first day couldn't have been much different than my first. Up down, up down, fall, get up . . . etc. But with one step in front of the other, one day in front of the next day they grew, they got stronger, and their muscle memory improved over time. They pushed their boundaries and pushed the human body to failure until, all of a sudden, the action that seemed impossible became possible.

I have some daunting news for you. You aren't going to be an expert on day one, two, three…you get the point. So here is where you need to make a conscious effort to understand success does not come right away, but it's easier to comprehend if you realize that no one, you and society looks up to, becomes a success right away.

People fall and then they get up again and each time they get up they are getting closer and closer to greatness. Body builders don't look anything like the way they do when they got started. They didn't go to the gym one time and start looking in the mirror and go, yep, that's it, I'm there. It is a grind, it is a process, and at points, you are going to feel things aren't moving fast enough. But trust me, if you are putting in the work, staying in the game and pushing your limits to "failure," you are going to keep getting closer to where you want to be.

John Elway, the iconic Denver Broncos' quarterback, had a phenomenal quote about being great. Overall, we are building a new version of you that is resilient and consistent. Consistency is one of the keys to taking your life to the next level. Elway said,

I became great by being good over a long period of time.

We are building consistency of behavior and attitude. Think about how important this quote is coming from one of the greatest of all time. Year after year, statistic after great statistic without being a champion, his persistence and hard work led him to end his career after many "close calls," with a championship to go out with two Superbowl Championships and MVP honors in his final game . . . Superbowl XXXIII.

OVERNIGHT SUCCESS IS A DANGEROUS MYTH

Often, we hear the phrase, "overnight success," and wish we could be that person, mostly because it fits a lazy narrative. It gives you an unrealistic goal where we think we can "strike it rich," without a ton of effort and rely on luck. I have a news flash for you, almost every "overnight success," has a much more intricate backstory than anyone realizes.

Restaurant owners are a great example in this day and age. With the advent of Yelp, social media and endless reviews from people who have no clue what it's like to run a restaurant, people have become ruthless in their wannabe Siskel and Ebert review process. (Siskel and Ebert are the most famous movie review twosome in history from the 70's-90's for you youngsters reading this book). Here's the deal, sometimes a restaurant deserves bad reviews, sometimes they don't. People are often too busy taking selfies with their food while it's getting cold and aren't always kind to servers, causing the servers to react poorly.

Regardless, this analogy serves as the perfect example of the concept of the 'overnight success.' I've had conversations with new restauranteurs that felt the need to vent about bad reviews and biting consumers head's off for not realizing how difficult it is to open a restaurant. Guess what, the consumer doesn't have to understand because they are just eating there, not opening one, the restauranteur is.

Even the best restaurant owners have had a bad review and have made a mistake. The best of the best, Gordon Ramsey, has even fallen victim to bad reviews. I've seen him talk about these negative blemishes he has had over his career that helped him to get to where he was. When things go wrong in the beginning, most try to fix their mistakes whilst taking responsibility for them. Through trial and error, things tend to improve over time, and then poof, "all of a sudden," the restaurant becomes a success. People then start to call it an overnight success because they have no idea about the struggle that occurred in the months and years prior because they are just hearing about it when it's "successful."

If you are one month, six months, or years into your business, job, or career and you are hoping for an overnight success story realize that concept is a BS pipedream. When you make it, to someone that didn't know the backstory and the struggle, people are going to think you were an overnight success.

So, to re-define failure, we must fully dispel the myth of overnight successes.

One great example and case study is Gary Vaynerchuk, or Gary Vee as you probably know him. Way too often, because of his brash nature and no-nonsense attitude, t-shirt, jeans and tennis shoes style, we think he's just an overnight success hotshot know-it-all who never knew what grinding it out and failing looked like. I have a news flash for you, he was NOT an overnight success. He grinded for over a decade to get to become the man you know now. And to be clear he hasn't stopped grinding and is going harder now than ever, but now he's in the spotlight and recognizable as a poster child for success.

Gary V took his semi-successful family wine business from $3 million in revenue to more than $60 million in five years after finishing college. He worked from early in the morning until late at night, seven days a week, and gave up having fun, partying and hanging out with friends. This was his growth as a businessperson. He did everything he could to become a success and turn that business into a huge success, and honestly didn't really get much from it but a crap ton of lessons and experience. People might think he was lucky because they only saw the end product. I encourage you to stop looking at just the end products and analyze the journey as the shiny object at the end, as end products provide an illusion that things can be easy.

At some point, he founded VaynerMedia, invested in several startups, helping them to become successful by sharing his knowledge in marketing and hard work, and then became one of the most sought-after keynote speakers in the world. Try and tell Gary V he is an overnight success and that he has never faced adversity and failure to his face. You're not going to want to be there for his harsh response.

Social media apps demonstrate other examples of the illusion of an "overnight success." Let's talk about Instagram for example. To many this can seem like part of a huge grouping of tech startups that achieved overnight success. However, Instagram is far from an overnight success. It was originally known as something called Burbn which was a super confusing check-in app for people that liked booze. There was little early traction up until the point the co-founder, Kevin Suystrom, noticed something that changed the trajectory of the company. He noticed that users were engaging in photos more than anything else. So, he simplified the user experience to photography with the ability to comment and "like."

Boom, they switched from Burbn to Instagram and soon after, it was acquired by FB for $1 Billion. Don't think this was an easy move for the company as Kevin received an intense amount of pushback when he made this decision. With the complications and algorithms of Facebook, the acquisition of IG has allowed Facebook to stay relevant with the gen Z and younger demographic. Its simplicity is what sets it apart and has made it arguably the most valuable tool of FB.

Fun fact, and maybe time to put this book down for a bit for a fun exercise if you so wish. I suggest making a list of all the companies, people, and businesses you may follow, idolize, or assume were an overnight success and then do some research on them. You will be astonished to see the backstories and you'll quickly realize there is NO SUCH thing as Overnight Success.

So, to summarize what we are doing in this chapter, we are re-training your mind, we are re-defining what it means to fail. I want you to forget all the preconceived notions you have in your head about what failure is. Ditch it. If someone calls you a failure, you say, "Thank you," and say you hope the same for them because that means they have given themselves an opportunity for greatness. Just know, true happiness and true success ARE NOT EASY, but trust me, the harder you push the limits the more it will be worth it.

I don't want you to feel daunted when I keep saying things aren't going to be easy. Remember Les Brown's quote here and I'll say it again.

If you do what is easy, life will be hard,
and if you do what is hard life will be easy.

Chapter 2

Discovering How to Double Down (Negative Progression)

Why the h*ll are we using a gambling strategy or concept to talk about life . . . sounds pretty dangerous and dumb if you ask me!

Well, let me tell you. Some of the greatest gifts and lessons we have in this life are from the places of the most pain. My father was a compulsive gambler, which is dangerous on its own merit, but adding in that I was raised right at or below the poverty line, it makes it even worse.

Twice before I was five years old my father gambled away our family savings in one night, which at the time was just a couple thousand dollars. Once it was a gift that was given to my mother and father right after I was born, and a few years later it was whatever we had from my mother's job.

My father's gambling addiction was not the only issue going on, in fact, he was also disabled with Multiple Sclerosis. By the time I was in my early teens he was using a wheelchair and by the time he passed away in 2014, he was fully wheelchair bound. He could not work past the time I turned five, and unfortunately at the time, he was unjustly fired by a hotel and casino called Circus Circus in Las Vegas, NV. They didn't have the same protections for handicapped or disabled people as we do now, and they were able to get away with it.

So, his only recourse was gambling, which is also interesting because he was legally blind in one eye and almost legally blind in the other . . . yet he still found a way to play Blackjack. I didn't know until I was much older that he played by a certain style of play and betting, and ironically enough, I found out by mathematically stumbling on the same technique that he used.

I remember it was somewhere around 2012 or 2013 I had finished working with my staff in Omaha, and a buddy of mine that had been working with me got a really hefty ticket that essentially ate up all the money that he had made while working for me. I felt horrible about it, and at the time, had the money to cover it, but he really didn't want it. On the drive home with a separate group, we decided to swing by a Casino in Oklahoma because I started thinking about what seemed to be a fool proof strategy and I was very confused why other people had never thought about this (news alert-I was not the first).

I started thinking in my head, if I doubled my bet every time I lost, I would always end up my original bet ahead. I could lose way more than I would win and I would still win. I tested it out on my phone on the "Blackjack app" and I would lose three, four, five, six hands in a row and in the end, I would still continue to build the amount of fake money I had in my fake wallet. I was like . . . "let's try this out in real life, the casinos are just off the highway."

I'll never forget it, I went in with my friend James, and I was giddy to try this out, and also had a little rush thinking that if it worked, I was going to be banished from the Casino for cheating. The philosophy was that I was going to have to reach into my pocket at times for a lot of money, but A) that's fine because I had plenty of money and B) if the sh*t hits the fan and this doesn't work, I can afford to lose $500 or $1000. That was one big difference between my father and me. He bet what he couldn't afford to lose. At this point in my life this amount of money was a non-issue, as my company was generating over seven figures of revenue, and I was operating at a decent margin… life was good.

Anyways, back to gambling, see diagram 2.1 in order to learn exactly how this method works.

fig 2.1 - How Negative Progression Works

Your Totals	YOU	the bet	DEALER
-$10	lose	$10	win
-$30	lose	$20	win
-$70	lose	$40	win
-$150	lose	$80	win
-$310	lose	$160	win
+$10	**win**	$320	lose

5 losses, 1 win = up one original bet ($10)

I sat down at the table with $500 in chips, and my goal was to double up my money and give my buddy $500 and walk away a happy and accomplished man. So here it goes . . . Bet $15, first-hand, lost. Bet $30, second hand, lost. Bet $60, third hand, lost. Bet $120, fourth hand, lost. Things were not going as planned, and fast. Fifth hand was the last of my chips in order to keep this "betting style," alive.

On this fifth hand I bet $240 and had already bet and lost $225 in about 5 minutes. In total, I was in $465, and as a non-gambler this was a lot and fast. The most I had ever gambled all at once in my life, prior was around $250. and that was just for fun, knowing it was "for entertainment purposes," only.

Needless to say, I was getting a little nervous. I mean, just because I could afford to lose it doesn't mean I wanted to. So, hand five, boom . . . I won, which means I was not just back to even I was up $15. Fast forward about thirty minutes and I've officially doubled my money and I was out. I grabbed my chips, ran to the cashier as fast as possible, thinking I was going to be escorted out of the casino by police. (Honestly, I was terrified that I had just broken the law and cheated the Casino – Hey, I thought I was a genius).

Turns out, I found out later that Casino's love people that play this way because most people who are only trying to make a few dollars and duplicate at $10 or $20 win, will have immense trouble reaching in their pockets when they need to for that $200, $400, $1000 dollar bet, and yes, that does happen very often. On top of that, tables are in place where, if you play this way and you have seven, eight or even nine losses in a row, you've gone over the table maximum and again... the house wins. Also, people have trouble settling a goal amount and sticking to it when they are winning and eventually one of the above scenarios happens and boom, house wins.

Although I did win, I STRONGLY suggest against utilizing negative progression in gambling, and I can use my father as that cautionary tale. Reluctantly, about two months later, I told my mom of my trip to the Casino . . . yes, I was almost thirty years old and had never mentioned any gambling activities to her. Even over two decades later, the scars from my father and his gambling run very deep.

Regardless, I wanted to tell her about this trip to the Casino and when I did, I told her how brilliant I thought I was, until I realized it was called "Negative Progression." She said, "Anthony, you realize that is how your father played right?" I had no idea, interestingly, this whole strategy that caused me a bit of joy in the moment is also what caused immense pain growing up.

Apparently, my dad always said the odds of not losing the fateful eight hands in a row that would push the limit of a $10 bet to over $2,500 was worth the risk. Turns out, however, that the odds aren't exactly "ridiculous." The odds of losing eight hands in a row is 1/170, and if you play long enough, it's bound to happen. This eighth loss is important because it is usually where you are now out of the table maximum range and for those playing with minimal money to start you are out of your bankroll. Bankroll is a term used by all kinds of gamblers that signifies the amount of money you have set aside to gamble with.

With all of this in mind, after I was born, my dad's family sent a couple thousand dollars to my mother and father as congratulations, and that was much needed to help us live. To make a long story short, eight losses in a row happened, and my father lost every dime.

On another occasion when I was three or four years old something similar happened with whatever savings we had at the time, and my father lost it all utilizing the same Negative Progression betting method. So please remember, this is a VERY dangerous betting strategy, and I don't recommend it.

With that disclaimer out of the way I want to get more into how I came to realize the philosophy behind negative progression is a really amazing way to look at life. With the philosophy that life has no "table maximums," and if you have the guts, you can always keep reaching in your "pocket," and finding the strength to double your bet and try another hand. Let me try and make sense of how I came to recognize this "double-down life strategy."

In 2018, I merged my seven-figure experiential staffing firm with another agency for no buyout and just a minimal percentage return from previous clients for the next twelve to twenty-four months, depending on the remaining contracts in place. It was time to start working on another venture that I had in front of me called #bethechange, but I'll talk about that later. With that, I was still sitting on a decent amount of savings, but there was a squeeze on my income, so I had to see if I could utilize some of my saved capital to generate money in other ways.

I attended a conference that included organizations teaching options trading. I got pretty excited about it, as it was very analytics and mathematics based, so I went to a weekend course. I picked up the basics and then did some extra learning and research afterwards.

Soon, I was trading options in the stock market with a few thousand here and there which led to decent gains, nothing spectacular, but I was definitely in the positive and I was learning at the same time.

Shortly after, I got a little more aggressive (some would call it greedy) and I was doing more options at a time with higher price points. To give a basic summary on options trading, you can purchase 100 shares of a stock at a specific price that allows you, based on many factors, a lower price, to own a much higher stake of stocks than you can "technically" buy. This gives great potential for larger gains, and it also gives much higher volatility and risk.

As I started to get more aggressive, I started to make mistakes, some big, some little. The one thing I noticed is that as I was learning I was doubling down on my mistakes and making sure I didn't make the same mistakes twice. Regardless, it was starting to get a bit more costly, and I was starting to get a little too loose and aggressive in my "trading," which was starting to resemble gambling more than anything else.

THE TURNING POINT

I was trading a very, very hot stock called TLRY (Tilray), it was a "pot stock" that was growing by leaps and bounds, not just weekly, but daily. It started out as an IPO (initial public offering) right around $20 to $30, if I remember correctly, and all of a sudden it started to make big jumps. In this kind of volatility one can make A LOT of money if you are in the options trading game. To this point, I had made mistakes, learned to take profits as they come, set metrics, learn what the volatility crush is, earnings season strategies and much more. I had definitely "learned," from a lot of mistakes, and here was my master class on mistakes which caused me to completely redirect my life after this big lesson.

Back to TLRY; I had made a risky trade overnight and it paid off, I had made about $2,500 on a $1000 investment. The next day . . . I got greedy and the stock did something called "go parabolic," and it jumped over a hundred points in one day from the high 100's to when I got involved again to almost $300 a share. I was on a lunch break at an event I was hosting, and I thought I could make a quick thousand dollars in a few minutes, so I got back in with this fast-moving stock and invested almost 11 thousand dollars in one option with a goal to sell it for a $1k profit in ten to twenty minutes (or less).

The stock hit $299 and apparently there was a huge amount of auto trade sell orders by people that knew way more than I did about stock manipulation. Instantly the stock dropped forty points (dollars per share) and the FTC shut down trading on the stock (which I quickly googled-and it's a death sentence for those "holding the bag." Holding the bag means those who still hold the stock when you know the stock is about to come crashing down.)

So, now I'm trying to figure out what to do when trading resumes fifteen minutes later, I was now down about $4k of my 11k investment and when it opened again I saw it bounce up a few points so I held steady until boom, it dropped another twenty points in a minute, so the FTC shut down trading on the stock again, and now I knew I was screwed. As soon as trading opened back up, I immediately cut my losses and sold for a $7,500 loss. Which was actually smart because that was the highest that stock would ever be again.

I sat there in semi shock; I mean I had lost a decent amount of money to this point but losing over $7k in under an hour was a new level of mistake. The thing I remembered my mom telling me about my father was that his biggest adrenaline rush wasn't when he was winning, it was when he was losing. That is the sign of a true compulsive gambling addiction. So, I sat there, collecting myself and almost got excited that I had made the mistake and that I would learn from it, and I would be stronger on the next trade as I watched my "bankroll," shrinking and shrinking and shrinking.

In this moment, I decided it was time to pause and reflect. I was no longer trading intelligently. I was trading twenty to forty options at a time worth upwards of 70–90k, all from my e-trade account on my phone. No intelligent trader, or human being for that matter, would ever think this was okay or a smart idea. It's not. I promise you that.

I started to weigh my options and think about what I was going to do next. I could take my remaining money, invest in a bunch of monitors and extremely fast internet, and start waking up at 6 a.m. after researching all night, and become a full-fledged day trader. I will be honest, to this day I know that I could have made the shift, and I firmly believe I would be a successful day trader. With all the lessons I learned, mixed with the decent relative success' while doing everything whilst being poorly equipped with only a friggin' phone, I have no doubt. Despite the losses, I was a bit of a natural.

With all of that said, when I started the business, I was working on at the time, #BeTheChange, I knew that I was focusing on a purpose greater than myself. I believed that with my background in speaking, emceeing and hosting, that my voice was meant to do something greater than sit at a computer and just "make money." I had said for a decade that my end game was to become a motivational speaker, author and someone who inspired people to find something special inside of them.

So, I simply made a decision to stop trading and begin to figure out what the h*ll I was doing with my company, and my desire to be someone that inspired people to take action and make change. That night I stayed up until 5 a.m. in a Jerry Maguire "mission statement," frenzy.

This failure over TLRY had allowed me to know what my niche was, what my core message was, and it was "The art of doubling down."

I realized that my very short-lived career in day trading, all the way to my whole professional life had been lived like negative progression. I had many more failures than successes, but I was somehow still ahead. How was that? Because every time I had failed, I had analyzed the mistake and made a mental note to never let that happen again. In a sense I was doubling down on the mistakes and often coming out stronger than before.

That's the key. Coming out stronger than before. It isn't about getting lucky; it's about being more prepared. I realized that everyone in this world is so afraid of failure, although inevitable, that it is an unspeakable and often too avoided subject. We shy away from it, avoid the lessons and just pretend like they didn't happen. Avoiding failure is the single biggest and most tragic mistake we make as human beings. It means we have to live through the pain of failure and get absolutely nothing from it.

I don't believe in having regrets, but if I didn't take risks, and if I didn't learn from my failures, I'd regret that awful decision. The great part, it's never too late to look back at our failures and learn from them. We shouldn't dwell in the pain, but instead try and separate our feelings and learn from these moments and become stronger, more equipped, savvier and better set up for our next success.

Chapter 3

The Double Down Lifestyle

I have to be honest, although the technique of betting is actually called negative progression, it's simply not as sexy of a moniker for something that is an actual bada$$ way of living life and thinking. I remember when I started meeting people in the public speaking world and they said, "Well, what would your keynote be called? I said, "Negative Progression." The advice I got from the veterans was overwhelmingly...well... constructive. They said if you were at a conference and five other people were speaking at the same time and you saw something titled, Negative Progression, would you want to go to that one?

In my head, I said, *h*ll yeah, that sounds fascinating,* but that's because it's something I already know. We have very little time to catch the attention of people in today's headline-driven world. So, I humbled myself a bit and realized the core tenet of negative progression is the idea to always double down on every loss, and this works beautifully in life . . . and let's be honest it has a much sexier ring to it.

So, now that you understand the gambling correlation, let's talk about it in relation to the way we design our life and in relationships to our path towards success and happiness. How do we make this a lifestyle? Why should we make this a lifestyle?

First off, we hear the words "double down," all the time. We hear it in politics, we hear it in sports, we hear it in business. At its core it means the person doubling down is reinforcing what has already been done or said. We hear, "Trump Doubles Down on . . ." "CEO of XYZ doubles down on . . ." Biden doubles . . . never mind, skip that one, "Tom Brady doubles down on . . ." Well, in Tom Brady's case, it's pretty much always doubling down on winning, but that's a different story. For the Brady haters out there, don't judge me. I'm not a superfan by any means, but let's be honest here, the guy was amazing.

Often when people talk about large companies, you'll hear them say they doubled down on a certain investment. This sometimes means it was already successful and they want more of something or that maybe it hasn't proven itself yet, but they are stacking the investment with the belief it's still going to be a smart play.

This is where I want to start with us as human beings. We need to double down on ourselves with the belief that, no matter the situations we are in or those that we have lived through, we still believe, in the end, that betting on ourselves will be a smart play.

We are all destined for successes and failures as we go through life, but the choice we make is how they affect us, and happiness is a biproduct of this. I've heard Gary V, whom I've mentioned earlier, say that the ROI (Return on Investment) in life isn't financial gain, it's not even perceived success . . . it's happiness.

Once we come to understand that life will contain more failures than successes, then we can move forward on taking advantage of the core understanding of how life works. This goes for happy and successful people just as much, if not more so than, as unsuccessful, miserable people.

NOTHING CHANGES IF NOTHING CHANGES

The concept is simple, often we sit around and expect or hope that things are going to miraculously start going well for us. I have news for everyone reading this; this is not how the universe works. The definition of insanity is doing the same thing over and over again while expecting a different result. We have to be willing to change things up.

Going back to a gambling and cards reference, sometimes people are repetitively losing as a group at a Blackjack table because the dealer is constantly getting good cards. It is typically good to have someone, or a couple of people, to sit out a hand. It changes the order of the cards, and yes, it's probably just a superstitious thing at this point when it comes to a "game of chance," but this is my story…and I'm sticking to it! In life, however, if you're having a run of bad luck, it means it's time to change things up.

When push comes to shove, you are in charge of your destiny. You alone can make a change. Remember the story from Burbn in a previous chapter. Burbn wasn't working, but part of it was working. That's how the idea of Instagram was born. It required a major pivot in concept. Imagine how hard that had to be to tell investors, "Hey everything you invested in isn't working, but this part is, so we are going to ditch almost everything and try a much simpler concept and see what happens." Now that takes some guts, but as we all know the phrase, "no guts, no glory!"

One shift can change EVERYTHING. What in your life is in need of a major shift? Do you need to change your schedule? Do you need to change your outlook on life? Do you need to change your overall attitude? Do you need to change your diet and overall health? In the end you may not see until later that these changes created the turn you needed in order to turn everything around.

The first major step of the double down strategy is to realize CHANGE is the greatest asset we have to create a positive shift in our life. Our willingness to try new things, new directions, new ways to attack life is what will ultimately be the guide to change our destiny for what the outcome becomes in our search for happiness.

So, now that we are willing to make a shift and have a willingness to change, how does this play into the double down lifestyle? First off, most of us simply need to start with the concept of the first chapter where we've redefined failure.

The concept of trying new things and being willing to take new adventures is paramount for us to understand this Double Down Lifestyle. We are no longer afraid of failure, so we can start to broaden our horizons in order to attempt a new direction in life.

There is a fascinating study regarding commercial fishing that backs up the philosophy that explorers and those willing to try something new are the winners in tough times. The study, by Shay O'Farrell and James Sanchirico from UC Davis along with Orr Spiegel of Tel Aviv University, examined the routes and results of nearly 2,500 commercial fishing trips in the Gulf of Mexico over a span of two and a half years.

The research discovered that those willing to explore new locations benefited far more than those that kept repeating the same places that were deemed "tried and true." This is a perfect microcosm of the COVID-19 pandemic in 2020–2021. During the study some of the prime fishing grounds were unexpectedly closed to protect the population of endangered sea turtles. Those that had vigorously explored prior had alternatives for other options when their usual fishing grounds were suddenly taken away. This mirrored what happened with the business closures of the pandemic. Also, when looking at the immediate impact of storms, the groups that had been explorers all along were not disrupted as much as those that had to scramble in the face of adversity.

If I haven't made this clear yet, I'll say it again . . . Life is full of storms, adversity, and failure. When we have a heart of exploration and a strong mind willing to be flexible and try new things all the time, we have given ourselves the capability for success in all conditions, not just when the waters of life are smooth sailing.

DOUBLING DOWN = SMART RISK TAKING

The great part about risk taking is that it opens up a whole new world of opportunity. The bad part is that the more risks you take, the more you set yourself for failure. This is where it's important to adopt the double down lifestyle. As you begin to take more risks, look at the failures and analyze them to see if there is a way to prevent the same kinds of failure in the future. These failures are making you smarter, more well-rounded, and more equipped for decision making as you progress forward.

As you continue to take risks and fail, you'll be able to start assessing future risks more carefully. This is where true progress happens. Having the know-how and ability to assess a situation beforehand, to see if it is a risk worth taking, is the true hallmark of a successful person.

I don't want people to take my word on risks, with the intention to keep throwing darts at a dartboard and expect this new amazing successful result. The analysis of the missed darts is the staple of the double down lifestyle. Over time, risks become less risky because you've made the mistakes and learned the lessons necessary to make your risks smarter and more informed. Any profession, especially those working as an entrepreneur, requires risk, but the idea of being a smart risk taker is what sets the person that understands these concepts apart.

Look at failure as something that is a navigational beacon of where we can go in life instead of a measure of who we are. That mindset shift will be a game changer in the way to approach risk and failure.

Although Mark Zuckerberg isn't my favorite person, he has one of my favorite quotes on risk taking,

The biggest risk is not taking any risk.
In a world that's changing really quickly, the only
strategy that is guaranteed to fail is not taking risks.

So, in order to be ahead of the curve, you have to be taking risks, but please understand a failure from a risk that doesn't become a lesson is the only thing that is a true failure.

This thought process can be summed up as trial and error. Risk taking is a critical element of having an effective life. Risk taking is best defined as "Undertaking a task in which there is a lack of certainty or a fear of failure." A true leader is typically in their position because they have the understanding that without an element of risk, nothing would ever be accomplished. No major medical breakthroughs would be discovered without trial and error.

We must make constant tweaks and course corrections in our lives in order to figure out what works. How do these course corrections happen? By making mistakes and having wrong formulas. Without wrong formulas there would not be right formulas.

Sir Alexander Fleming made the discovery of penicillin almost by accident, which is a funny story in and of itself, but the fact that it was "discovered," in 1928 but not used to treat a civilian patient until 1942 shows the importance for trial and error. I do hope most of our trial and error in our life doesn't require fourteen years to come to fruition, but you get the point. Trial and Error are necessary for progress and all these errors are progress disguised as what we call failure.

For those that want the quick story on the discovery by accident, Fleming went away on vacation and when he returned to his laboratory a month later, he discovered a fungus had developed in a stack of Petri dishes containing bacteria. Essentially, he had left his workstation a mess, but it turned out this fungus killed the bacteria that was growing near it, while bacteria in the dishes farther away were unaffected. His team of Ernst Chain and Sir Howard Florey helped by conducting clinical trials over the next decade and more to prove the hidden ability of penicillin to kill bacteria. This is now the common cure for Staph, Scarlet Fever, pneumonia, meningitis, and many serious infectious diseases.

Now, I'd like to provide another anecdote that will add a layer to this analysis of the failure thought process. I, personally, am allergic to penicillin as are many other people. I can die if it's given to me in these instances. Although Penicillin is a miraculous discovery, it is far from perfect and thankfully, as people started to have adverse reactions, they didn't just keep giving it to people that would get sick or die from it. This is where analyzation of failure and doubling down becomes an important philosophy. Fortunately, other medicines were developed for those that can't safely utilize penicillin, like Azithromycin and others. So again, failure bred ingenuity and progress.

DOUBLING DOWN ON HARD WORK

Let's be honest. We've clearly become softer as a society and need to start realizing there is something to be said about being tough, being able to deal with things going wrong and being able to take a beating and keep coming back. Now to be clear, this isn't me saying emotions are bad, and safe spaces or only for pansies... I'm simply saying there is a time and a place for letting it out and showing sadness and there is a time to use the crap in your life going against you as the fuel and as the fire to fight back and reach new levels.

I'll get more into mental toughness later on, but right now I want to make sure I'm properly relating the importance of understanding how hard work integrates into the doubling down lifestyle.

Part of doubling down isn't just learning from your mistakes and getting back in there. It's also doubling your efforts. When you find out what you've done wrong, and you have your next goal set in your sights, you don't just give it another go. *You go for it.* Doubling down also means giving double the effort once you re-direct and pivot. The key element that makes people successful is the fact that when they fail, they bounce back harder, faster, and stronger.

The great part about "hard work," is that its definition is unique to each of us. The way I'm outlining it for you right here is that when one thing hasn't worked out in life and you've been handed a loss, winners get back up more determined and hungrier than before.

After failures, people tend to become more timid, shell shocked and afraid of the next mistake, and deathly afraid of the next failure. This is the complete wrong way to handle a failure. Look at it like this; you have the opportunity to try again, you are still alive, you are still kicking, so what was so bad about the failure? So, why not just go for it? Understanding that it's not going to kill you when you fail is the first step to start going hard towards your next move.

Ultimately, the thought process behind hard work and doubling down is that your definition of hard work should fully support your concept of happiness and success. To break it down, the double down lifestyle means getting knocked down and then right back up again, like a rabid Pitbull, hungrier and more determined. Let failure be your motivation and fuel, not something that depresses you.

The closest thing I can tell you about regrets in my own life was when I lost almost 700k worth of future business in one day. For the first several years of my staffing business I was consistently making the right moves. I had miniature blips on the radar, but I felt as though, with my hard work, consistency, and a quality product I was almost infallible. Turns out I wasn't.

I had been pitching two clients and had landed them both. We were working out the final details of approximately $400k with one and $300k with the other. For a business that always stayed steady with just over $1 million in revenue yearly this would have almost doubled my business just like that. I had hired an extra person and spent hundreds of hours of planning and negotiating.

In one day, the roof caved in on both of these new accounts, with one of them going away within a month of launch because the woman sold her business and disappeared in the middle of the night. Dead serious, that's how it happened. In the other instance, the account was stolen out from under me because I was told the account was mine by a higher up. I had literally written the slides in their deck on staffing and helped them land several big accounts. I thought we were just ironing price, when it turns out...they were bidding it out at the same time, and someone undercut the price to a ridiculous amount. I'll talk more about this a bit later in the book. But the point is that, in one day, I lost $717k of business just like that. POOF.

Before I go any further, as a side note, I want you to know the client that undercut the business came crashing down and I ended up picking up the slack, as they completely failed on the program's staffing...but who's counting?

I said this was the closest thing I have in my life to having a regret. So, what do I regret? Losing the business . . . no? Do I regret not seeing the other business being sold coming? NO! I have regrets at the way I handled it. I sulked, h*ll I even cried at times, for two weeks. I still had a successful seven-figure business, but I felt like a fraud. For years I'd given advice to those that wanted to start a business, I gave advice on how business and life worked and all of a sudden, I faced a massive failure and I shut down. I just felt as though everything I had told people over the last several years was bullsh*t because I was a failure. Unfortunately, the only thing I was failing at was not knowing to get my a$$ off the ground and get back to work.

If I wanted to grow my business, sitting around and moping for two weeks wasn't going to get the job done. Be upset for a day or two...sure. That's human. But, allowing it to get to me like this was such a waste of time. These kinds of failures happen, and in the end, it made me more aware, stronger and more inquisitive with clients, so why was I so upset? I was so upset because at the time I didn't properly know how to handle FAILURE, and in that moment, I was a failure. This is the closest thing I have to regret, but the great thing is, I know years later that I can't change the way I reacted, but I know I won't act like that ever again, and that is where I turn that L into a Lesson.

Not having regrets, and not moping in failure is the ultimate trait of someone living the double down lifestyle.

So, what are the pillars of the double down lifestyle?

1. Be willing to make a change.
2. Take risks
3. Progressively take smarter risks
4. Hard work
5. No regrets
6. Failure is fuel

You're probably saying, "Wait what is this failure is fuel concept?"

Let me blow your mind for a second . . . failure is necessary to reach new heights, like fuel in a rocket ship. A study published in the journal "Psychology of Sport and Exercise," looked at what happens to us after we fail. The findings concluded that, although a setback hurt self-esteem, it didn't affect actual performance. When combined with other studies, it turned out that it was the opposite, it has a long-term effect on lasting success. The key was in *how* the athlete emotionally dealt with the setback.

The key is turning the failure around into improved performance. This relates to a view in psychology called "Cybernetic Control Theory." It essentially says that as the pressure of failure is put on our nervous system, our brain functions, in a sense, to balance us back to center. They use the example of a thermostat and a furnace. A thermostat senses the temperature in a room and then the room temperature is compared against that. If the room temperature is below the temperature it's set, the furnace is ignited, and the heat comes on. Essentially the brain wants to get us back to the desired temperature.

With that said, if the temp is too high, the air conditioning will come on and cool down the room. The same can be said for my story about losing all the business in one day and how I handled it.

Another example is the 1991 University of Las Vegas Nevada Men's Basketball team.

What happens when you aren't tested, aren't pushed, and don't know what it feels like to fail? A hint; you are unprepared for adversity.

If anyone is a college basketball fan, the late 80's and early 90's belong to a couple teams, and one of them being the UNLV Runnin' Rebels. I was born in Las Vegas and through my childhood that was "my team," to say the least. In 1990 they won the National Championship and in 1991 they were the hands down favorite to take it again, especially as they entered the tournament at the end of the season. They were undefeated, and untested.

This should mean it was a clear path to victory, but instead their lack of dealing with adversity and failure proved to be their Achilles heel in the semi-final game against Duke. They were tested and it came down to the wire, and without knowing how to deal with being down, and being pushed, they failed miserably. They looked flustered and confused, and they put up a terrible final shot. The lack of failure and the fuel that goes along with it caused them to come up short for their ultimate goal of a championship.

So, remember, everyone loves a comeback story, and comebacks aren't possible without failure and the fuel to feed the fire to actually make the comeback. This mentality now completes, "The Double Down Lifestyle."

You are dismissed… next chapter.

Chapter 4

Flipping Losses into Wins

In life the only way to win in the long run is to take losses and turn them into future wins. Sounds simple, and if you stay the course, it is. Remember this thought process and it will all start to make sense. What defines us in this world isn't the days where we wake up when all is well, and we take on the day with ease. It's the days where we have to drag ourselves out of bed, face the failures of the past and present, push harder in the face of adversity, and we succeed despite the odds stack against us. This is what defines your life and your destiny.

You've probably heard the phrase, "What doesn't kill you makes you stronger." The origin of this quote is a phrase from the nineteenth-century German Philosopher, Friedrich

Nietzsche. I love the thought process that this quote and this mentality on overcoming failure and never giving up is a centuries old anecdote on toughness and perseverance. Throughout Nietzsche's book of Aphorisms, he talks about taking serious accidents to his own advantage, and how, with lessons learned, he was made stronger. To summarize, suffering builds strength.

The question becomes, how does this mindset relate to flipping losses into wins?

I like to use concrete analogies such as working out, body building and building strength. Growth in the muscle fibers comes from pushing weight close to our max or when we run to the point of complete exhaustion. That is when the body creates more muscle, a reaction to adversity—become stronger.

Let me go further into one part of this. What happens when we lift *light* weights to muscle failure? When lifting light weights for a high number of repetitions in a single set, fatigue arises.

WARNING: TECHNICAL TERMINOLOGY AHEAD, BE PATIENT, I'LL MAKE IT MAKE SENSE.

This fatigue occurs primarily through the accumulation of metabolites inside the muscle. This accumulation has been proposed to interfere with the actin-myosin bindings, and in this way reduces the ability of each individual muscle fiber to produce maximum force. The onset of fatigue also reduces the muscles maximum contraction velocity.

Therefore, in order to keep force at the required level, as we approach muscular failure, the central nervous system increases the number of motor units that are recruited. The greater number of fibers that are activated compensates for the lower force being exerted by each individual muscle fiber.

As muscular failure approaches, the central nervous system recruits all the available motor units to help. The full motor unit recruitment at a slow contraction velocity then provides sufficient mechanical loading on the muscle fibers linked to the high-threshold motor units such that are stimulated to strengthen and grow. THIS is how lifting light weights to failure produces something known as hypertrophy. Hypertrophy, simply put, is exaggerated growth or complexity.

Thank you to Chris Beardsley for doing the *heavy lifting* on this concept in his article on training to failure.[1]

So, how does this "hypertrophy," relate to the philosophy of "what doesn't kill you makes you stronger" and flipping losses into wins? To put it simply, you are testing yourself, pushing yourself to the brink where your physical ability no longer can succeed because of total exhaustion. This is the point where you are mentally fighting until your body has given up and, in the end, grows at a much more accelerated rate. Over time, it's building muscle and creating strength and resilience. You didn't die during the work out, but you tried really hard, you pushed to ultimate muscle failure, and you survived with the reward of muscle growth.

1   Beardsley, Chris. "What Does Training to Failure Actually Achieve." Medium. November 5, 2017. https://sandcresearch.medium.com/what-does-training-to-failure-actually-achieve-2837460c5f0f.

This concept is consistent in other parts of your life. Think of your brain and your heart as a muscle, that, when tested, and when life continues to dish out all the bull-"crap," you continue to push forward using lessons from your failures and all of the pain you have been through. Through this you are creating mental fortitude and strength that gives unparalleled opportunity for growth. This growth creates strength and raises the ceiling for success and potential.

This of course requires a positive attitude, and a willingness to keep stepping up to the table of life, realizing there is always inherent risk in constantly taking risks in facing trauma and inevitable occasional disappointment.

There are a few different similar definitions for the term "hypertrophy," and I chose this one because I like the "complexity," portion of this definition. On top of the growth, it also creates complexity. This means that through hardships, through losses we are creating layers and levels that make us a more complex human being. One with more facets, more skill sets, more intrigue into the person we are, and the person that interacts with others on a daily basis. We are a higher version of ourselves when we take these losses and build that unseen muscle mass in our heart, guts, and head.

SOMETIMES YOU GET "BLACKJACK"

The way I described negative progression also comes with an example that is all about timing. The more we keep getting back in the game, learning from our losses and continuing to double down, the more we give ourselves the opportunity for the universe to give us good timing. That is exactly how negative progression works. Every time we win, no matter how many losses, we always end up a step ahead of where we started. Essentially "one bet" ahead.

I want to change that up for a second and show another alternative. If we've lost a few hands in a row—say we started with a $10 bet, and we have lost four times in a row—we are at a loss of $150 with a current bet of $160. Winning this hand puts us up the original $10, but there is one other alternative that can happen in our favor. We can win by means of a dealt Blackjack or "21." When this happens, it's a bit of luck, but in life, in order to get lucky . . . we have to keep playing and keep trying. Many tables give a bonus to a dealt Blackjack with a payout of 2 to 1. This means this $160 bet would pay $240 back, meaning not only are you up the original $10 you are up another $80. BONUS!

This translates to life that despite all of those losses, if your win comes with a little bit of luck and good timing, you have put yourself in contention to not only come out ahead but to skip some steps and have a big win. We talk all the time in sales and in business about "big wins." This is essentially what this is, a big win, perfectly timed, using the losses in the past into a bigger win. If you aren't constantly doubling down on your bets in life you aren't giving yourself the chance for this really satisfying level of success. I've provided a diagram to show exactly how the above bet works in Blackjack, and I'll let you apply this metaphor into your only life.

fig 4.1 - How Negative Progression Works
WHEN YOU GET DEALT 21 (BLACKJACK)
3/2 PAY ON BLACKJACK

Your Totals	YOU	the bet	DEALER
-$10	lose	$10	win
-$30	lose	$20	win
-$70	lose	$40	win
-$150	lose	$80	win
-$310	lose	$160	win
+$170	WIN/ BLACKJACK	$320	lose

5 losses, 1 win with Blackjack =
up one original bet + HALF FINAL BET
$10 + 160 = $170

Flipping losses into wins also matters in your relationships and personal life. In the next chapter I explore the philosophy on micro and macro failures more thoroughly, and will add another layer, but for now let's talk about flipping losses into wins on a day-to-day basis with the people around us.

Relationships come with inherent failures built in, often on a daily basis, but each day we have an opportunity to take these failures and turn them into something positive. If we walk around on eggshells with our significant other, spouse, or even close friends then we'll never push the boundaries of a relationship to make it extraordinary. It will always feel like it's missing something. Why? Because we are not giving 100 percent of ourselves, we are simply just existing together and not being our true self.

Sticking with the norm and being complacent can make a relationship feel stuck and stagnant. This willingness for failure as a couple and in a friendship opens up new opportunities. No matter how amazing a relationship is, without growth and change, it's going to become boring for both parties. Human beings need ups and downs. We need peaks and valleys for us to truly feel as though we are alive. A flat line is just that . . . a life with no heartbeat, no passion, no true bliss.

So, try to be romantic once and a while, it may end up feeling embarrassing, or dinner might get burnt, or you may end up pulling your back out doing the horizontal mamba . . . who knows! But you tried, and sometimes it will be that one spark that keeps the relationship going. There is nothing less passionate than the same routine all the time. There is nothing less sexy than the words, "It's Thursday, 8pm, and this is when we had in our calendar to have sex."

We have to be willing to try something new at times, and we also have to be willing to be ourselves.

This doesn't mean on occasion we don't sacrifice for the other person or do something that is a tradition in a relationship. This means there has to be some kind of deviation from the normal course that sometimes includes some risk of embarrassment or failure.

Also, this can help you realize if this isn't the person you are supposed to be with. If it is relatively early in a relationship, and the person you are with makes you feel like, most of the time, you have to act like someone else, it probably isn't going to work. If you never get to put your foot down for your own needs, it may be time to fold your cards and walk away. That being said, sometimes it just takes communication of the sense you try to put your foot down and your feelings and beliefs get rejected in order to truly give it a fair chance.

The longer we wait to test out failure scenarios, the harder it will become to leave a relationship. You don't want that. Far too often when I talk to people that have broken up years into a relationship, I hear that they should have broken up much sooner. Most people get too committed and too comfortable to even end a relationship that doesn't allow for someone to be themselves and for both parties to grow as people. Remember, relationships are only successful when you are sure of who you are, and the other person loves you for that person.

So, be yourself and be willing to risk losing someone in order to truly find the happiness you desire.

I do have a small caveat here…this does not mean to not be willing to grow. There is a place where your significant other is wanting you to grow as a person. Being yourself is not the same as being too stubborn to become the next, more positive version of yourself.

So how is this actually flipping a loss into a win you might still be asking. Let me give some examples. On a larger picture I know so many people who left a relationship that wasn't working and immediately found the right one, utilizing the failures from that relationship and the character traits that didn't work with that person to find the significant other that was their perfect match.

My significant other is a perfect example. She had been off and on with a guy for several months before we started dating, and the whole time she knew this wasn't the one, not even close for that matter. She lost herself and found herself at times. Although she kept bouncing back and forth, she finally figured out it was time to leave the situation. She knew exactly what she wanted out of her next partner, and after some prayer, things worked out pretty quickly.

Amazingly enough, after less than a month our paths crossed, and I fulfilled most parts of life that her previous boyfriend was missing. If she didn't push the envelope near the end of that relationship, whilst asking for specifically what she wanted and it not being delivered, she may have continued the relationship too long, and we wouldn't have been together.

I want to be very clear, I'm far from perfect, but I filled the exact needs emotionally, spiritually, comedically, and motivationally she needed out of her next partner.

Inside of a relationship the same things can be said. Communication is one of the top reasons for break-ups and divorces. Since you've read to this point, I think you understand it's incredibly difficult, if not impossible, to get better at anything without making mistakes. Some people avoid tough conversations with the person they are with in order to avoid conflict. Without the tough conversations that may lead to big, blow-out arguments, a couple can never learn more about the other person. So, although, in that moment, these arguments seem rough you have to realize, sometimes stuff has to come out. You just have to learn to NOT make the arguments personal. Don't attack character, attack issues.

The key to this is a willingness to actually have a conversation after things have cooled down. This is where you analyze, with an open mind and open heart, what went wrong in that moment of communication. What needs weren't met, and what wasn't properly communicated. This way, with proper, open-minded conversation, you can learn more about each other and also know subjects or behavioral traits for the next time something similar comes up.

You are flipping communication failures into future communication wins because you are constantly learning through the mistakes. If you never have any debates or arguments, you don't have the highs and lows and communication missteps you'll never be able to grow as a couple. Bottling this up and avoiding the conflict will eventually lead to harboring animosity for things that could be fixed if you would just take the chance to have these conversations.

The other common relationship mistake is not having a balance between work and home. I want to be clear, as an entrepreneur I have a jaded belief system on the terminology "balance." I believe that for those willing to put in the work to build their business or build something special, they will have more balance in the long run instead of one moment in time. I call this delayed onset balance. If you want to be a true entrepreneur balance cannot be on the top of your list of things that are important in life. It is even harder if you want a partner that supports this. Just remember, you can't make others believe in you until you fully believe in yourself.

When it comes to unhappiness at a job, this often spills into home life and friendships. You become strained as a human being and it reflects right on the people you love. Sometimes people need to find a side gig or business that allows them to fulfill some needs separately or they need to bust their butt at work or get a promotion or a raise. If you don't take the chances for failure at a job or in your own self-business life, you'll never know what potential you have. You must be willing to take risks for yourself.

The greatest analogy we can use here is being on an airplane. Before take-off, the flight attendant gives the spiel about putting your mask on before your children's. This is because, if sh*t hits the fan, you need to be able to help. If you are so concerned about the people around you and forget to take care of yourself when you're needed the most, you'll be without oxygen. So sometimes, in order to flip losses into wins in a relationship, you have to double down on yourself!

COVID-19 AND 2020

The year 2020 was one h*ll of a doozy, I think we can all say that. Even those who flourished had to deal with a complete upheaval of normal life. This was the year of the pivot; some sank and some excelled.

Companies like Tesla, Amazon, Peloton, and more, EXPLODED to new heights because they fit the mold of lockdown-proof, and in many ways, especially Amazon and Peloton, were literally built for people forced to stay home. Peloton may not have planned for the long haul however…and has had some major struggles as of late.

I also have many friends in the world of course development and coaching, who took what they already had in place and absolutely killed 2020. Media companies made the switch from in-person events to online events, and that exploded. A company that I use for all of my live shows and events, called StreamYard, ramped up their footprint in the industry as a perfect alternative to Zoom for live broadcast.

It's like Warren Buffet once said, "Be Fearful when others are greedy and greedy when others are fearful." In a year like 2020, if you had the ability to do something and took advantage of it, you thrived. Food delivery businesses found a way to work around mandates, and not only made a crap ton of money, but also helped keep small businesses afloat. Investors who had the guts to invest at the bottom made windfalls of money in the calendar year.

The way people flipped the loss that was 2020 into massive wins was by changing everything we thought about business. Every opportunity that was presented needed to be considered, as there was so much uncertainty. Things that may have been duds in the past were exactly what was needed in what was a very odd year.

Disney plus was a great example for the Disney brand on how to pivot, shift and thrive. With movie studios and theme parks becoming shuttered, they needed something really special to stay profitable. With smart investments in programming, like signing Hamilton and understanding the importance of children's programming with kids being stuck at home, they gained 86.8 million subscribers in the year. At $6.99 a month and that much of a subscriber increase, you can do the monthly revenue and you'll see how huge that was.

Unfortunately, small business was crushed in 2020 since many were not COVID-19-proof. If a business' main lane involved leaving one's house, it tended to fail, with good reason. In this case, to turn that loss into a win, business owners needed to survive in the moment and find a way to cut costs and turn to other revenue-making streams. In the long run, it was a huge win because, if you could survive with external business' that still profited during the pandemic, you came out the other side with two money-making businesses. These CEOs are in an amazing place right now because they double downed on life and found a way to re-invent themselves. Now they have become more multi-faceted and able to withstand the worst of storms.

My company, #BeTheChange, that I founded in 2016 with very little traction and use, increased its follower size by forty times in 2020 because we saw a need to take on tough conversations about news and politics. We shifted from just positivity to inciting people to "Be the Change," they wanted to see in the world and to learn more about politics. I sent a FB message to a gentleman by the name of Kash Lee Kelly that went viral for a social media post he made. In a short period of time, we ended up becoming fast friends after he was a guest on the show. It literally ignited our growth and allowed for something of value that wasn't there before.

Ultimately, it was the long game that allowed people to thrive in the year 2020, and those who didn't double down for their success and livelihood sank like a ship to the bottom of the sea. Riding it out simply wasn't an option, doubling efforts and testing failure was the only way to set yourself up for a win in 2020.

I had a friend that was in the entertainment industry who, as he got older, decided to completely change things up in his career and began . . . wait for it, painting. He does have his real estate license, but unfortunately even that was a struggle, especially in his part of LA. Admittedly, early on our friend group just assumed he was bored out of his mind and his paintings were decent, quirky and honestly pretty cool. As the pandemic continued, he kept working on it, and despite everyone probably thinking he had lost it, he found so much joy that he kept working tirelessly and, in the end, got better and better.

By the end of 2020 he was selling his artwork as a sustainable living and even creating custom-painted shoes and also selling those for good money as well. So, not only was he now fulfilled with joy in his hobby, but he had also begun replacing the income he was losing.

To use a reference I learned earlier, for those that doubled down many came out ahead and some even hit Blackjack, and they catapulted so far past the original bet that it was unreal. The year wasn't for the weak of heart, but it was for the warrior willing to do whatever it took!

Chapter 5

Explaining Micro
& Macro Failures

I n life, we have failures that course-correct what we are doing daily, little losses, and in some cases, much larger more glaring "failures," that some deem as almost impossible to overcome. This chapter is going to be another dose of mind restructuring by analyzing how detrimental a failure is. I like to utilize these two categories, micro and macro failures, to describe the losses we take on in our life.

Some things seem like the end of the world, and that the walls have officially closed in, but if you restructure your thoughts to shrink the size of the mountain that is the failure, you have a more obtainable path to overcoming the negative. Once you are able to shrink this rocky terrain down, life will get easier and easier, and overcoming failure with ease will become second nature. This will also make you less risk averse.

WHAT ARE MICRO AND MACRO FAILURES?

Typically, when we think of "micro" and "macro," we tend to simply think of them as descriptions of things that are either "big" or "small." And while this is partially true, it doesn't tell the whole story— it's not THE BIG PICTURE.

So why do we hold these simplistic definitions for these two terms? It's probably because when we do hear the words "micro" and "macro," we hear them in the context of economics. MICROeconomics and MACROeconomics, two terms that give us the impression of big and small. Microeconomics deals in the "little things," the economic behaviors of individuals and households, while Macroeconomics deals in the "big things," the economic behaviors of states and nations. Remember, though, these are simplistic definitions and don't get to the crux of the difference between the two terms.

In fact, "micro" and "macro" differ more in the METHODS behind their use than just the easy definitions of "big" and "small." The difference is METHODOLOGY more than anything else. Now, believe me, I know that can sound as esoteric as all get-out, so let me continue breaking it down by shifting from economics to real-life examples of failure. But keep in mind that while micro and macro failures may seem easy to distinguish on paper (micro failures are "small" failures, macro failures are "big" failures), it's more about the methodology behind the use of these terms.

Methodology is defined as:

1. The underlying principles and rules of organization of a philosophical system or inquiry procedure
2. The study of the principles underlying the organization of the various sciences and the conduct of scientific inquiry

How does this apply to failure? And how can we apply this when determining what is or is not a micro or a macro failure? What this means is that we have to determine what constitutes a micro or a macro failure before we begin to label our failures as either. Then we have to use the principles we've found to see which label applies best to any given failure in our lives. Essentially, we are conducting an experiment, analyzing our failures to find the truth behind the varying levels between micro and macro. I know this may seem confusing now, but I promise you, it'll make much more sense as I analyze a sample list of real-world, real-life, down-to-earth failures that we're all familiar with.

Let's begin by jotting down a list of random failures that we have either all experienced, come close to experiencing, or have avoided at all costs.

- Forgot to take out the trash
- Failed a test
- Divorce
- Lost a job
- Didn't get a promotion
- Flunked a test

- Woke up late/missed an appointment
- Missed a flight
- Didn't close a deal or sale
- Lost a house/foreclosure
- Bankruptcy

These are obviously the basics. Of course, we could list many, many more (there are a PLETHORA of failures out there!), but to keep it short and sweet, we'll leave it here. However, I recommend that you grab a piece of paper and write down each of these failures and even add examples of your own, whether big or small. Then, on a separate piece of paper draw a line down the middle, creating two columns. At the top of these columns, write "MICRO" above the left one and "MACRO" above the right.

What we're going to do is conduct an experiment for each failure on this list. We'll analyze each one and see if they fall under the category of a "micro failure" or a "macro failure." If the failure is one which we could easily bounce back from, get up, dust ourselves off, and try again, we'll put it in the MICRO column. But if the failure is an end-of-the-world, absolute catastrophic disaster that you can't come back from, then we'll place it under the MACRO column. I encourage you to do this first by yourself, then come back to see how similar your categorization matches up after a proper, methodological analysis. You may be surprised at how your current mindset towards failure takes away from your ability to grow and, ultimately, contributes to your level of risk-aversion.

* * *

All right. So, you've gone through the list, added your own, and divided them up between the MICRO and MACRO columns. Let's go over them together and see where each one falls after careful scrutinization using the methodology we've been discussing.

Let's start with the easier ones and work our way down to those that are harder to classify.

FORGOT TO TAKE OUT THE TRASH

The easiest one on our list. Forgetting to take out the trash is obviously annoying; the trashcan is packed or overflowing, a small fight could break out. If you live with someone, maybe there's a lingering smell, but this is easily remedied. Simply take out the trash when you get home. Most of us realize that forgetting something is bound to happen and we don't beat ourselves up over it. The lesson learned is easy to remember, set an alarm, take out the trash when asked, or take it out once you think of it yourself in order to avoid any distractions. Clearly, this is an example of a MICRO.

WOKE UP LATE/MISSED AN APPOINTMENT

Once again, an easy answer. Waking up late or missing an appointment is easy to get over and easy to fix. Again, setting an alarm, and remembering to check your calendar regularly are simple solutions. Sometimes, when it comes to waking up on time, the issue stems more from your mindset. For example, no one wants to wake up early to exercise (it's the last thing I want to do first thing in the morning!).

But the solution is still easily fixed: maybe place your alarm clock in a place that requires you to get out of bed to turn it off. By the time you're out of bed, you might as well stay out of bed. But even when you do wake up late or miss an appointment, it's not the end of the world. Mark it down as a MICRO.

MISSED A FLIGHT

This is an interesting one. If given very little thought, it appears as if this may be similar to missing an appointment. But with some consideration, you realize that missing a flight can create a chain of events that could alter your life in major ways. If the flight is for business purposes, missing it could mean missing out on a new job opportunity, a business deal, or an important meeting. Now, it's true that almost everyone in business understands that travel issues happen, and they are often willing to figure out an alternative. But even in the situation where this isn't the case, stay positive and keep your eye out for a reason why it didn't work out; maybe the universe was trying to help you.

Interesting Story

Seth MacFarlane, the creator of *Family Guy* and *American Dad*, was scheduled to be on Flight 11 on September 11, 2001. His publicist accidentally gave him the wrong time, and when he arrived at the airport (a bit hungover, in his words), the flight had already boarded. Little did he know that this small accident had saved his life, for only a few hours later Flight 11 had been hijacked and flown into the World Trade Center.

You never know when a little mistake can alter or save your life. The lesson is to always stay positive and next time take precautions. Plan in advance, double-check flight times, adjust for traffic, etc. Missing a flight isn't only something that you can bounce back from. In Seth MacFarlane's case, missing a flight allowed him the opportunity to bounce back because he's still here. We've got another MICRO (albeit complicated) on our hands.

FAILED A TEST

Failing a test can seem pretty disastrous at the moment. If the test was an important factor in your final grade, then it can seem as if you may not advance to the position you'd like in your career. But I assure you, having the highest GPA or the top score on the LSATs, or the highest score on any other standardized test for that matter, will NOT change your future unless you let it. With every failed test comes a strength you can acquire. A failed test is a chance to learn from your mistakes, and you can CHOOSE to not make those same mistakes again. How you finish is always more important than how you start. Also, I'm forty and can count on one hand how many times someone told me they were a valedictorian of ANYTHING. In the long run, it just isn't a factor in real life.

Think of it this way: If you score moderately across the board on ten tests that are all equally weighted, your average is still moderate. A bunch of 70 percent tests still equals out to an average of 70 percent. But if you have one FLAT OUT ZERO and the rest are around 90 percent, your average is 81 percent or better. A failure is a chance to learn, not an excuse to give up . . . MICRO!

FLUNKED A CLASS

To any student, flunking a class can seem like a death sentence for their future. Flunking has so many ramifications: extra expenses, re-takes, an inability to move forward in your major. There's no doubt that flunking is a setback. However, the phrase, "Every setback is the setup for a comeback," isn't just a corny line—it's the truth. When I have the pleasure to talk with students and graduates that tell me their stories about sticking with their majors, retaking courses, and advancing through their majors, they all describe the experience as having made them stronger and better. You're always better on your second attempt than on your first.

But truly, the stories that capture my attention the most are those in which the student realizes how little their heart was actually invested in their major. Flunking a class that was a pre-requisite for future classes TAUGHT them to re-evaluate what they really wanted. It gave them pause and the chance to try something new. I've heard multiple stories where they changed course and didn't look back. They left pre-med, went into law or marketing, or even vice versa—and it made all the difference in their lives.

Flunking is simply a chance to analyze your future and proceed with new vigor. Ultimately, it can be a blessing. But even if it's not, the setbacks you'll face are just that, SETBACKS, not complete stagnation. I promise you that. With that, knock knock . . . who's there . . . MICRO.

DIDN'T CLOSE A DEAL/SALE

Oh boy, I've been here before. I talked about this in a previous chapter, and I'll say it again. In 2014, my business was all primed up to double its profits. I had two $500K+ accounts that would take me into the $2M revenue category. Unfortunately, I lost both new sales—on the same day! Months and months of work all down the drain. Trust me, I can empathize firsthand with what losing a deal feels like, but I can guarantee you, a positive attitude will always lead to bigger and better things.

Let's recap, the positive of losing one of these accounts revealed itself within just a month! The first client was a nationwide staffing program with field managers and brand ambassadors for a coat brand. They were forcing me to cut my budget by hundreds of thousands of dollars, but, in the end, chose someone else due to a $17K difference in the budget. If I had known that this $17K would make or break the deal, I probably would've come down, but you know what they say, que será, será, (what will be, will be).

However, here's the payoff: the client that undercut us wasn't overly organized and the event turned into a complete cluster-you-know-what. Usually, my company specializes in making events like this work, but the events kicked off in late February, just before my father passed away in mid-March while I was hosting a two-week-long event. If we'd been staffing the whole program, I would've been in a world of hurt and turmoil. It'd be an experience I'd look back on as the worst time of my life rather than simply the month my father passed away, something we all must face at some point in our lives.

But even if this hadn't been the case, and it had just been another lost account, I would consider it a chance to analyze why we didn't land the sale. It would be time to do a postmortem and review with the client what we could've done differently. And if you find yourself in a similar situation, this is a time to show gratitude and courteousness to the client. In the end, they may be so impressed at your willingness to accept defeat and improve that you may become their first call for a bigger account. Essentially, missing out on a sale is barely a failure in my estimation. It's a very important part of the growth of your business . . . so MICRO!

DIDN'T GET A PROMOTION

Now we're getting into trickier territory. Many people might classify this under MACRO. Understandably so, too. They'll say how they fought for weeks, months, years to position themselves in just the right spot for this well-deserved and much-needed promotion. We start to see how this borders on MACRO because, I mean, what do you do now? You might as well put your tail between your legs, go back to work, hang your head and give up, right? OF COURSE NOT!

Similar to what we've discussed above, this is certainly not an excuse to give in, it's a chance to re-assess. Perhaps, after some consideration, you realize this isn't the job you're supposed to be at. Maybe it's time to take your talents elsewhere, somewhere where they're appreciated and compensated fairly. Or maybe, when you truly give it some thought, the new job with its new responsibilities would have taken you away from things you value more, such as your family. Or maybe this just isn't the promotion that was meant for you; there could be another just around the corner that you're much better suited for.

Once you alter your thinking and stay positive, you'll realize this is your shot to make an adjustment for your future, not to submit. I encourage you to look up the life of Vera Wang to see how not getting a promotion leads to true greatness. Vera Wang failed to become the editor-in-chief of Vogue and doubled down on her life to become the design director for Ralph Lauren. Two years later she got the idea to start a bridal boutique and as we all know, the rest is history. A promotion is merely a question of timing, position, and situation, all of which are relative—not absolute doom and gloom. MICRO!

DIVORCE

Here's another tricky one. Many people will consider divorce to be the end of their love-life, the disintegration of their family, or the last chance they'll have to start one. I'd love to tell you that second marriages have a higher success rate than a first marriage, but the stats don't lie. Second marriages do, in fact, have a higher percentage of divorce than first marriages. HOWEVER, this is not a stat that should scare you. There are too many intangibles here to ignore!

Now, I'm not a certified counselor, but I'd love to work with divorced couples because it's such an opportunity to change who you are. One possible explanation for the rise of divorce rates during second marriages is that most humans tend to make the same mistakes over and over again. But if you review people who, after their divorce, take the time to learn from what caused their first marriage to fail, they're far more prone to happiness in their second marriage. They know how to avoid the situations that got them in trouble in the first place. It's a chance to learn what you like and don't like in a partner, an opportunity to set boundaries for yourself and work on those parts of yourself that make you attractive and desirable.

Some people learn they're happier alone, while others find a freedom they never felt during their first marriage. What I can promise is that, after you've handled the children and the home situation (if these are relevant), you've been armed with a whole new artillery of self-awareness bullets. But only if you choose to accept it. I'm not going to lie, it's going to be hard—but it's far from the end, especially if you treat it as a learning experience. Bottom line is, you're still here! So . . . MICRO!

LOST A JOB

Here we go, we're getting into the real nitty-gritty, tough-as-nails "failures" that many of you, I'm sure, placed in the MACRO column. And I don't blame you. Most of us have been laid off, fired, or let go for one reason or another at some point in our lives. The financial toll that it takes can, in its immediacy, seem like the end of the d*mn world, making this appear MACRO as all h*ll.

But before we consign to this label, let's think of this another way. Like the other reasons listed above, let's keep the concept of changing our perspective ripe in our minds. When we maintain a positive attitude, we can more readily accept ideas such as, "things were meant to happen this way." Losing a job is frightening because we see it as just that—a loss. But we should instead see it as CHANGING a job.

Maybe there is an opportunity about to come your way that a job would hinder you from taking. Maybe a family tragedy requires you to stay home for a few months. And even though this may sound strange, this is a chance to filter out those friends who are only there for you when things are going well. Friends that don't have your back when the worst befalls you are not friends at all. Cutting those friends from your life is nothing but a benefit to you.

But perhaps the true benefit is in the lesson your kids glean from the downsize in your life: the true value of a dollar and that you can still rise from failure. This is a much better lesson than you can possibly teach from constant success. Don't you want your children to learn to make the best of any situation? Teach through action and embody this attitude yourself. Learn from your mistakes, make changes where they need to be made, and open yourself to new opportunities. You may find that a better job is right in front of you. We have another MICRO!

LOST A HOUSE/FORECLOSURE

This is a rough situation; I can't deny it. But hey, you're reading this now . . . and that means that you're not completely without. You're not out of the fight yet! Chip and a chair (poker reference), right? In all seriousness though, in this situation, you have to downsize, get creative, and overcome. Looking back at the housing crisis from a decade or so ago, there were people losing their houses left and right. Some were overextended, some had a run of bad fortune, some lost jobs, had bad relationships, missed opportunities.

However, even with a country full of people who don't know the powerful secret of positivity, who don't have the willingness to fail, it's a simple fact that we, as a nation and those in the housing market, are FAR better off economically than we were ten years ago. When we get down to brass tacks, if you keep plugging away, keep working, keep chugging along, and don't overextend, you'll find a home that fits in your budget. And you'll know from experience to give yourself a cushion if hard times befall you once again.

It should also be noted that sometimes it wasn't the cost of the house that led to foreclosure. Sometimes it was a series of work decisions that put you in a tough spot. It's important that, in these dire situations, that you analyze ALL the decisions that contributed to a bad outcome. If you go through all the possibilities, you'll mitigate the risk moving forward. Everyone has different limits, different thresholds on what they can handle. This is your chance to learn about yourself and learn how much you can take on.

So, take a guess at what label we'll put this under? Well, Les Brown said it best, "If you can look up, you can get up." This means this is a very, very tough MICRO.

BANKRUPTCY

Surprisingly, out of all the major "failures" we've seen, this can be one of the most positive. One of the great things about the American system is that when you take on a challenge and put yourself at risk, but unfortunately end up facing a major debt because of it, we have many ways to declare bankruptcy that don't make your life impossible. These opportunities give you a chance to restart and try again, but now with all the knowledge you gained from that initial failure. It's understandable to feel dejected if you're struggling with bankruptcy, but remember, this dejection is a choice. Bankruptcy doesn't define you; it gives you a second chance. So, this may be a shock, but. . . . MICRO AGAIN.

* * *

Hopefully, you're beginning to see the pattern here. Many—if not all—of the "failures" in our life that we perceive as unbeatable are actually, at their core, micro failures that can be overcome with positivity, a change of perspective, and a willingness to accept the change that comes with failure.

Actually, this reminds me of a funny story: One time, after a speech I gave on this subject, someone approached me and told me that there was one failure that was technically a macro failure. I replied that I was listening. "If you're a bomb technician," they said, "and you pull the wrong chord." "BOOM," I said. "The exception that makes it a rule," and good for a little chuckle . . . unless you're a bomb technician, and in that case I'm sorry if that hit too close to home.

With that being said, though, it should be noted that any of these failures can be considered MACRO. Of course! But remember what kicked off this section. What got us talking about micro and macro failures to begin with? Ideology and methodology. What classifies a failure as either micro or macro is a consequence of your reaction. It's a question of self-responsibility. It's up to you to not make mountains out of molehills. In other words, it's about perspective and your perspective is 100 percent your choice. So, make the right choice and overcome.

I once overheard a woman at the hospital giving a pep talk to her elderly parent who was in poor health. What she said was powerful, it stuck with me, and I refer to it when times are difficult. She said, "If you're still here, your track record of getting through tough days is 100 percent."

Chapter 6

Overriding Failure 101

*If you're still here, your track record
of getting through tough days is 100 percent.*

I f you wake up each morning, then you have another chance to bet on your goals, dreams, and future. Overriding Failure is an amazing concept that will work wonders in your life if applied the right way.

Imagine a life in which you have a switch on your nightstand, or in your desk drawer, or in your car that, when pushed, the nightmares of life just dissipate. Think about that for a second, could you imagine if the Staples "Easy Button" was a real-life item that could do what the old Calgon ads suggested and simply "take you away?" (Quick note: Calgon are bath products for all my younger readers).

Unfortunately, in the real world, there is no kill switch. Life happens…and then it happens again…and again…and it's not always positive and it is definitely not always fair. However, one of the things that I've learned and shared throughout this book is that doubling down is a concept that helps you take failures and flip those losses and prolonged defeats into wins.

And the truth is, if you want to develop your own internal override switch to overcome the nagging and tormenting failures that everyone faces, then you're going to have to train your mind to process failures. Think of your mind as a strainer, the kind used in cooking. When you make pasta noodles, you drain them through a strainer once they've finished cooking. The strainer has holes that are small enough to keep the pasta from falling in the sink but large enough to allow the water to flow out.

Many people who face failure want to throw everything in the sink, the water along with the noodles. But like the old expression, "don't throw the baby out with the bathwater," you must become efficient at not dismissing the failures in your life because of embarrassment, pain, loss, rejection, or fear. If you're going to understand success and experience victory on a constant basis, you'll have to develop your ability to override the most hideous aspects of failure and embrace the lessons learned in the heat of adversity. You cannot let failure trick you into giving up your pasta or your baby. It sounds like a joke (and it sort of is), but I am serious! Failure can drain the life out of you if you're not careful.

The concept of overriding failure only comes after we've learned how to recognize failures and then distinguish between micro and macro failures (as I discussed in the last chapter). There are some people who'll give up too early because they mislabel a micro failure as a macro failure. And then, there are others who go on denying their failures entirely! Once you feel comfortable with these two steps, we can begin to develop your kill switch and train your brain to override any failure life hands you.

Well…actually…before we do that, I should clear something up first. It should be stated.

that there are times in which all the micro failures you're experiencing are signs that it's time to quit and move on before those failures become macro. I understand that the bulk of what I talk about is sticking in there, staying the course by utilizing failures, but there is a time when it's no longer right.

I refer to this as when doubling down goes wrong. A while ago, I was conducting a webinar and, finally, someone asked the question, "when is it time to give up?" A fantastic question with an easy answer, right? I was about to say never, when I realized there's an element of pride that can get us all in trouble. He had asked me because he was in trouble in the tech business he'd started. He sounded like he was over it, exhausted.

I asked him if he still woke up in the morning passionate about his company, if he was still excited to follow through with the mission. Disregarding his lack of funds, I wanted to know if he still *loved* the idea, the backbone, the foundation of what he was doing. And…his answer was muddy, which meant, in my opinion, that the "override" on this situation was understanding that "moving on" is sometimes the right direction.

It's not "quitting," it's simply shifting focus to something you're passionate about again. Life is too short to waste time working on companies or ideas that are exhausting you emotionally, physically, and financially. There are times you have to bite the bullet and give different jobs and companies a shot. Otherwise, you'll never realize your full potential. You'll never know what you were put on this crazy earth to do without failing at a bunch of different jobs and ideas.

With that understood, I think I've made it clear how much raw power is latent within knowing how to override properly. When someone yields the power to override their failures, they can truly do anything. It's clarity of thought, it's being in the present. But those who wish to override their failures must know *how* to clear their minds, *how* to be in the present, if they truly want to move on and put the past behind them.

If you want to have this ability, you must learn the lessons, make the changes, override and progress forward. I can tell you till I'm blue in the face to learn, learn, learn from each mistake and each failure but, at some point, you have to take the blueprints and move forward on your own, without beating yourself up for previous mistakes.

So, you may be saying to yourself now: "All right, Anthony, I get it. Doubling down, negative progression, micro and macro failures . . . it all makes sense. But how in the h*ll am I supposed to just *move past* my failures?"

It's true. Failures can seem like such a heavy burden. And even though the concept of negative progression may make sense to the logical part of your brain, the emotional side may still have a hard time moving beyond failure. We often associate failure with negativity. This is a habit, though, that needs to be broken. Restructuring our way of interpreting failure, as discussed in the previous chapter, will help minimize this negativity, but how can we truly overcome that habituated emotional response?

Alcoholics often talk about the "habit" of drinking. For example, anxiety or depression may arise in their system and, in order to quell that feeling, they turn to the bottle. Over time, the desire for alcohol becomes directly associated with these anxious or depressive thoughts. The habit forms and embeds itself in their daily life. Many alcoholics have revealed that breaking this habit begins through "restructuring" their minds. What this restructuring often begins with is self-compassion through emotional control.

Well, overriding failure is another process of restructuring our minds. After we've developed the ability to properly distinguish micro and macro failures, we must then develop the habit of controlling our emotions. Always keep in mind that the negative emotions that you feel after failure arise only out of habit. And just like any bad habit, this too can be broken by keeping a steady eye on our emotional responses. There are, of course, many ways to hone this ability, but I've listed here three of the strongest methods to achieve this skill: Open-Mindedness, Don't Let Them See You Sweat, and Mental Fortitude.

OPEN-MINDEDNESS

The strategy of open-mindedness is a tad nuanced, so listen up and listen carefully. The word "open-mindedness" is often associated with looseness, absolute acceptance, and soft feelings of hugs-for-all. I want to say that we should move away from this. Open-mindedness is not about total acceptance of others. It's not even so much about other people as it is about you and your mental state when you've been dealt a difficult hand. Open-mindedness is a way to strengthen your mind and build a tolerance for that which you may initially perceive as negative.

Let me explain because even "being strong in mind" is often misunderstood. As the twenty-first century rolled along, our cultural interpretation of a "strong mind" (in a male) began to morph with the phrase "toxic masculinity." This is where I'd like to see a change occur. By "strength of mind" I do not mean to imply that we should suppress our emotions and act as if everything in our lives is perfect. (We especially should not be doing this if we are, in fact, unsatisfied with our lives!)

For decades, we men have been told to keep our emotions hidden, to "act tough," and hold the stoic expression that says, "Everything is fine just as it is." And yet, as many times as we were told this, we were never taught *how* to toughen up. We were thrown into the world with the simplistic advice of "be a man," as if that would give us the necessary skills to deal with all of life's hardships.

All of us know that this is a tragic way to teach men how to react to the world; the rising suicide rates among men tell us as much. However, with that being said, I want to add that medication should be your *last* resort and expressing yourself and talking to someone is a great first step. And it's this act of talking with someone that actually leads to what I really mean by "open-mindedness."

I'll tell you a little story: a while ago, I was at a leadership conference with a group that was . . . well, let's just say that, when it came to dealing with life's crappy dealings, they tended to have a softer and more sensitive approach than I did. But the key for me in this scenario was to remain *open-minded*. I knew not to judge and to keep my ears open. And I'll admit, it was difficult. I've always been the guy to label things like "safe spaces" as BS, a concept built for weak people. But this is exactly what I mean by "strength in mind": mental strength and discipline come when you admit to yourself that YOU DON'T KNOW EVERYTHING.

More often than not, when you actively listen to other people, you can gain new perspectives on how to deal with difficult situations. At this conference, I had a conversation with a younger man in which I continually argued against the idea of "safe spaces." But what I realized was that, deep down, I had a latent problem with feeling vulnerable. It dawned on me that this "tough guy" persona was, at its core, hindering me from seeing where I could grow. It was actually making me *mentally* weaker.

After this conversation, I understood what a safe space was. It wasn't, as I previously thought, a random corner for a weak person to scream, yell, and complain about their problems. A safe space is a locus of communication. It's a place where you can share your thoughts, be open, and also listen, such as a men's group, or a therapist's office, or even a private room with a close friend. In other words, a safe place is a place of growth, a place where one can learn how to control one's emotions and wisely "toughen up."

So, admittedly, yes, I am a "tough love" kind of coach. I am not the loose kind of guy who blindly accepts the ones who scream and complain in a corner. No, absolutely not. But I'm also not just a "tough love" coach who simply says, "be a man," "toughen up," and that's the end of it. Restructuring our minds to break the bad habit of viewing failure as a negative requires us all to listen and open up about our vulnerabilities. We must not be mentally weak and block our path of growth to keep up the "appearance" of toughness.

To be truly strong, we must admit that we do not know. And this perspective applies to our failures. You may say that a failure means FAILURE. But truly think back on how many times a failure led to an avenue of opportunity. This is what it means to be open-minded. Keep an open mind and you will be granted a horizon of possibility, instead of a barren landscape.

I always have to remind myself that the only person 100 percent wrong in a discussion is the person that thinks they are 100 percent right. That goes for any communication, and sometimes a tough persona creates a stubbornness that is detrimental to growth.

DON'T LET THEM SEE YOU SWEAT

The next method of overriding failure piggybacks nicely off the last concept. Because while being open-minded and vulnerable is important, the key to vulnerability is in knowing when to show it. Everyone and their mother have come across those who will take advantage of you the second they find out what your weaknesses are. So please, please exercise caution when choosing who to open up to. But don't beat yourself up if you find out too late that you've trusted the wrong person. We've all done it. And we should learn from it so that we can avoid those people in the future.

So then, what's the lesson? How can we recognize the signs of those who'll take advantage of us? Well, it's not easy. They manipulate by masking their intentions behind false compassion. However, you can cut off this approach from the get-go by "not letting them see you sweat." I'm sure you've heard that phrase before. It's a quality that you need to adopt to progress in your career and access your inner leader. It's the ability to set the chaotic world aside and keep your cool, even in the face of catastrophe. This gives you the appearance of a leader, which is often all you need to keep predatory people at bay.

And on top of this, if you're able to stay calm when the sh*t hits the fan, you'll find that people will want to listen to what you have to say. This chapter is about controlling our emotions, and sometimes that can be achieved once others already believe you to be someone in control. In other words, this strategy is a bit of "fake it till you make it." If you act calm, the people around you will calm, which will then *actually* calm you. It's a vicious but positive cycle.

And it works because leadership is about setting an example.

Leadership doesn't come from a loud proclamation, "I am a leader!" but instead from setting an example for people to follow. It's a well-researched fact that we're naturally drawn to leaders who display an ability to face adversity with little to no stress or emotion. When a manager is acting as chaotic as the environment around them, those willing to follow that person are usually also full of drama and emotion, which then feeds back into the environment! In that scenario, what you're left with is an army of emotionally charged loose cannons firing willy-nilly at everything that moves. This is not only bad for business, but also for life. And it's often the reason why businesses and their teams fail to reach their next level of growth.

However, I would like to add one small caveat. This is the exception that makes it a rule. If you do find yourself in a chaotic situation and your client, boss, or manager is in the midst of a frenzy, sometimes acting too calm can be infuriating. It can appear as if you don't care. So, adjust for situations in which you have to match the energy of your client with the same fervor and expediency. Put on a face to show you have the same sense of urgency. But on the inside, remain calm and logically work out a plan.

To keep within the theme of gambling, maintain your "poker face," don't let the others see you sweat. It'll not only protect you, but it'll probably be a big factor in how far your business goes.

MENTAL FORTITUDE

Mental fortitude, the essence of being "strong in mind." There's quite a lot to unpack in this method—more than you may think. I'm going to keep this section relatively short, and in a future chapter, I'll dig deeper into this topic.

But what I will do is this: dedicate this section to David Goggins. If you don't know who David Goggins is, I highly recommend looking into him. Goggins is an ultramarathon runner, a triathlete, motivational speaker, and all-around bad *ss. He's blunt, to-the-point, all tough and no love. But, hey, sometimes that's what you need. So, what I want to do is use his story and his messages to teach you how to gain strength . . . from challenges.

His first lesson? Every day, do something that sucks first thing in the morning. Why? Because even if it's temporary, even if it's small, it builds mental toughness. Start your day with a cold shower, add a 100-yard sprint to your workout, or tackle the day's hardest task first. All of these are a shock to the system that builds resolve and makes the rest of the day an easier endeavor.

Goggins talks about "callousing" your mind by making uncomfortable choices and fighting through the pain. It's only through pain that real growth can occur. Chasing pain, Goggins says, allows you the chance to learn about it, see through it, and conquer it.

It probably doesn't shock you, but Goggins knows a thing or two about pain. He failed at school, the military, and basic jobs. He was overweight and, by all definitions, considered himself a failure. But it was when he saw an ad for the Navy Seals that he realized the core issue he was facing actually came from within: he was giving up too quickly, he wasn't pushing himself enough. It dawned on him that through his whole life, he'd been running away from pain, fear, and uncertainty—and yet discomfort still found him. At that moment, he decided that he would stop running away from discomfort. He would instead run towards them. Without this realization, David Goggins wouldn't have become the inspirational legend he is today.

And Goggins's story ties in with the last thing I'll mention in this section. He tells us that we should surround ourselves with champions, with people that we aspire to be. If you want to soar with the eagles, your inner circle has to be made up of eagles. The people we associate with are the people we learn from. They challenge us and they remind us of the strength we need to complete the tasks at hand. The stories of champions are inspirational; they teach us, firsthand, all the techniques for overriding failure. Having them around is like taking the contents of this book and injecting it into real life. In fact, we should talk about that next. To override failure, you should familiarize yourself with inspirational stories of tough, strong-minded, strong-willed champions.

Chapter 7

Overriding Failure
Through Inspiration

G reatness doesn't come from thin air. Greatness doesn't come from luck. Greatness comes from a steady dedication to a process, a method of course correction to keep you heading in the right direction. Those who have achieved great things were not merely FATED to do so, and their "eureka moments" didn't happen on the first try. No, they had to face failure time and time again, adjusting their process until they figured out how to overcome their mistakes. They weren't simply destined for greatness. They made a habit of accepting the inevitability of failure and pushing through until they "got it right." Thinking otherwise on your journey to greatness will almost certainly lead to the worst possible outcome—giving up, QUITTING.

If you really want to change things up, create progress, create something absolutely kicka**, then you have to always be pushing the boundaries of failure. Over and over and over and over . . . Greatness may not be predestined, but failure certainly is. Sorry to break it to you but it's like Rocky said, "It ain't about how hard ya hit. It's about how hard you can get hit and keep moving forward. How much you can take and keep moving forward. That's how winning is done." Failing over and over gives you the opportunity to be first, to innovate, and win.

But even if we take a look at the Rocky quote, it doesn't quite explain why failure is so important. As advice for handling failure, this boxing analogy has been used for ages. And while inspiring, it seems to just barely miss the mark. In other words, it's incomplete.

If you were actually in a boxing match and a powerhouse left hook knocks you on your butt, what would you do? Get up, dust yourself off, sure. But you shouldn't jump right back into the fight! That same left hook would come swinging just the same and flatten you time and again. No, you'd take a moment to yourself, analyze their movement, consider why that punch landed, and make adjustments to avoid the same mistake.

And if you get knocked down from a different punch, then you analyze again and make the necessary changes. You eventually get so good at knowing what is coming you now have the opportunity to counterpunch (in the ring and in life). Only from an ANALYSIS of failure can greatness be achieved.

It's science! What's the first thing you learn about the scientific method? You test, method after method, until the results change. Nothing new or innovative is accomplished without some kind of failure. Just think of the first brain surgery. How well do you think that went? It may be a bit of a shocker, but—surprise, surprise!—it didn't go over so well. And the percentage of successful brain surgeries wasn't that great for quite a while. That is until, over the years, progressive adjustments were made to keep improving on the failures. Unless it's 2020–2022, then we just do the first thing Fauci says, and science goes out the window... but I digress.

But failure is not only important in the realm of our careers. Failure makes us more complete people. When we fail, we learn to recognize and empathize with those around us who are also being put through the wringer. And when we learn to overcome failure, we learn how to impart this knowledge to those we care about. Failure makes us better friends, better family members, better salespeople because it teaches us how to relate to others. Yeah, I know, failure sucks, but d*mn it, if it's not one of the most important parts of life. Without it, we'd be less compassionate, less empathetic, less understanding, each of which are the "balls to bones" qualities necessary for success and greatness.

It sounds strange, doesn't it? We've been so preconditioned to avoid failure that coupling it with success sounds totally nutty. But failure and success aren't polar-opposite foes, they're friends. They walk hand in hand, one always leading to another. Those who have achieved great things know this. And as I stated earlier, they made a habit of accepting that with success comes failure. It's not failure we should try to avoid; it's giving up.

Sometimes this can be hard to remember when confronting failure. In fact, many of the lessons I hope to teach in this book can be nearly impossible to enact when life is beating you down. But this is why I wanted to write this chapter. Because in the throes of failure, your will can feel so weakened that you lose all motivation to move forward. It's in these dark moments that you begin to consider giving up, settling with failure rather than overriding it. In these moments, your strength of will needs a boost, a shot of adrenaline straight to the veins. But if it can't come from within you, where can it be found? Well, my friends, the answer lies in the wisdom and stories of those who have already achieved great things. Motivation can be found through INSPIRATION.

Back in 2003, researchers Todd M. Thrash and Andrew J. Elliot wrote a research paper on the nature of "inspiration," giving it further definition in the field of psychology. One of their findings was that inspiration is "evoked rather than initiated directly through an act of will." It's an energizing feeling, they say, like a bolt of lightning from above that strikes us. And that energy from inspiration's lightning bolt surges through us, propelling us with drive. The participants of Thrash and Elliot's study found that, when inspired, they felt this drive led immediately to strong feelings of . . . (drumroll, please) MOTIVATION!

Bingo. We got it. When you just can't seem to will yourself into getting back in the game, analyze the inspiring stories of great, admirable people. Within their stories, you'll find numerous examples of personal demons, unexpected pitfalls, bad luck, mistakes, and failures. Sometimes (maybe even most of the time), you'll discover these admirable people faced problems you could never imagine overcoming yourself. And yet they did. This realization doesn't minimize your own problems, but instead, it should give you the vigor to rise above them. That is the purpose of inspiration. By analyzing the accomplishments of those you admire, you vicariously enter their shoes and override their failures with them. The strength they had then becomes yours.

Have you ever watched a movie like Rocky or Ali and, as the end credits roll, feel so pumped, like you could conquer the world? That's the feeling of inspiration taking hold of you. Search for that in the stories of real-life, admirable people. Analyze them and you'll be granted an endless well of motivational energy!

However, there's one small caveat. Motivation alone isn't enough to overcome failure. Remember the boxing analogy from earlier? Getting hit only to get back in the game immediately afterward is just going to lead to another blow to the head. Sure, inspirational stories can empower you with energy. But that energy is worth nothing if you don't know how to use it. So how do you learn how to use it? Well, you've already been given the answer. Maybe you've noticed, but I've been careful to use the word *analyze*—"ANALYZE their stories; ANALYZE their accomplishments." Inspirational stories are like a prerecorded boxing match of the greatest fighters that ever lived. And if you want to be a boxer yourself, you'll have to take a deep look into how the greats bobbed, weaved, and jabbed their way to victory. Study their technique and you'll uncover all the moves you'll ever need to override any failure that comes your way. You truly will be unstoppable.

Now, admiration is a personal feeling. Who and what inspires you can only be determined by you. But there are some examples of universal greatness that we, as a whole, can all agree deserve our respect. Their accomplishments speak for themselves and their stories of overriding failure are worth our attention. So, I'd like to spend the rest of this chapter highlighting a few of these stories. But with that said, I'd like to encourage two things:

1. Look more into the famous examples. The deeper you dive into their lives, the more you'll find that their personal struggles mirror your own.
2. Find your own examples. As I said, admiration is personal to you. The most inspiring stories are those that speak uniquely to you. Think about who you admire (famous or not) and learn as much as you can about their life story. I guarantee you'll never forget it and you'll always recall it when life gets hard.

But before you do any of that, let's go over some famous examples of true inspirational strength and drive.

MICHAEL JORDAN

The story never gets old, so we have to start with the absolute GOAT, Michael Jordan. As a sophomore in high school, he trained day in, day out to try out for the varsity team, which he desperately wanted to be on. But . . . when it came time for the varsity coach to choose players from the sophomore class, the team was already packed with seniors. Any sophomores chosen would just be substitutes for the seniors. What the team needed then, the coach decided, was size over talent. So, the sophomore the coach selected wasn't Jordan, who was only five feet, ten inches, but Jordan's friend, who was six feet, six inches. Jordan was devastated. His coveted varsity position was taken from him, and instead, he was placed on the JV team.

To Jordan, this was a failure. But he didn't just sit on the bench and sulk. He used this "failure" as fuel. Fortunately for him (and for every basketball fan), being on JV gave him much, much more playing time. Instead of a substitute, he became a starter. And because he felt he'd been passed over, he practiced, trained, and played with a chip on his shoulder, as if he had something to prove. Without overriding that "failure," who knows if Jordan would be the icon he is today? That failure sparked something in Jordan that eventually changed the course of sports history forever.

Whenever I was working out and got tired and figured I ought to stop, I'd close my eyes and see that list in the locker room without my name on it, and that usually got me going again. (Michael Jordan)

CHARLES SCHULZ

Next up is one of the most influential cartoonists of all time. If you like *The Simpsons*, CALVIN & HOBBES, or GARFIELD, you have this man to thank. Yes, it's Chuck Schulz, the creator of the PEANUTS cartoon. In his early life, Schulz loved to draw, often sketching out small cartoon caricatures of his dog, Spike. And not only was Schulz talented as an artist, but he had a set of brains on him too. In elementary school, he skipped two half-grades, excelling very quickly in his studies. But by the time he reached high school, he was the youngest one there. He felt underestimated by everyone around him, students and teachers alike.

One day he brought a couple of his drawings to the high school yearbook committee. They depicted two characters, one named Charlie Brown and the other, Lucy. The high school yearbook committee, however, couldn't find the humor or entertainment, so they rejected him. A few years later, Schulz would take these same cartoons to publications and studios, hoping to receive at least one acceptance letter. Everyone, including Disney, rejected him. He wasn't deterred though, saying that he was getting closer and closer after each failure.

Eventually, in 1950, the PEANUTS comic strip was accepted by and appeared in seven newspapers. At its peak, the revenue from the PEANUTS licensing and cartoon generated over $1 billion every year. Sixty years after Schulz's attendance, the same high school that initially rejected his drawings erected a five-foot-tall statue of Snoopy in its main office.

OPRAH

Do I even need to introduce her? She's Oprah! Of course, you know her! But what you may not know is that Oprah, in 1976, was offered a position as a co-anchor for the six o'clock news on Baltimore's WJZ-TV. This was only her second job as a news anchor. Prior to this, she'd landed her first job in local media as an anchor for Nashville's WLAC-TV, where she was both the youngest and the first black female anchor. In her early twenties, Oprah was already killing it! But failure soon struck (as it so often docs), when after just seven and a half months at WJZ, she was let go as an anchor and demoted to lower-profile positions at the station. She was, as the station said, not the right fit. Turns out, it was Oprah's compassion for the stories she was covering that led to her demotion. The station tried to separate her from sticking so diligently to the stories she covered because she would so often get involved. Little did they know, this is what makes Oprah, OPRAH. And this wouldn't be the first time a news anchor position didn't work out.

Oprah had this to say about another job that didn't work out: "I once went back . . . after covering a family that had been burned out and brought them some of my blankets and stuff. And the assistant news director . . . told me . . . that if I did that again and they found out about it, I could be fired, because I was involving myself in other people's stories. Which is true, you're there to cover the story, not get involved in it . . . "

But it was that passion to get involved and make an impact that paved the road to Oprah's gargantuan success. She's a media billionaire, the host of the highest-ranked TV show of its kind, and inspiration (and producer) for shows like Ellen, Dr. Phil, and Dr. Oz. Now if only Oprah could talk more about this and less about systemic oppression, just think about how much greater her impact would be... sorry I had to say it.

J. K. ROWLING

J. K. Rowling . . . the Writer Who Thrived. While I'm not personally a Harry Potter fan, the story of its creator is rife with life lessons. From failure analysis to keeping the passion alive, Rowling's rise to international fame is a great source of inspiration and learning. Having always wanted to be a writer, she came up with the main characters of her now-beloved series in 1990. But the writing of her novel ground to a halt with the passing of her mother, who passed away the same year. Rowling dealt with this blow by channeling her pain into the novel's plot, pushing the story forward as much as she could. But finishing it didn't get any easier, as shortly after her mother passed, she married an abusive husband. She separated from him, taking their young daughter with her to stay with her sister. This, however, left her in poverty, bankrupt, and on welfare.

Though this situation would topple most people (and who could blame them!), Rowling kept at her dream of becoming a writer, finalizing the first draft of *Harry Potter* in 1995.

But, as we all know, life doesn't let up so easily. Even with her book completed, it was sent to, read, and rejected by TWELVE different publishers. Rowling still doesn't give up. And I'm sure she thanks her lucky stars she didn't because the thirteenth publisher gave her a chance, who gave her one piece of advice: get a day job; there's no money in children's books. Do you want to know how much Rowling is worth now? Over one billion dollars . . . from children's books! And her impact on the culture? Incalculable.

In her speech to Harvard graduates in 2008, she had this to say about her failures:

You might never fail on the scale I did.
But it is impossible to live without failing at something
unless you live so cautiously that you might as well
not have lived at all—in which case, you fail by default.

I just read this quote to myself out loud…twice, and you should too.

SYLVESTER STALLONE

Earlier I mentioned a quote from the one and only Rocky Balboa, the cinematic model of the victorious underdog. Admittedly, I'm a huge fan of the character, so the story of his creator, Sylvester Stallone, is one of my personal favorites. It's no secret, but Stallone's portrayal of Balboa came from a very intimate place. His early life was filled to the brim with all the grime and ugliness that life has to offer. For a period of time, he was homeless, sleeping at the New Jersey Port Authority Bus Station. He saved up for a small accommodation, and when he couldn't afford to pay the bills, he had to sell his dog just to turn the lights back on.

During this time, he wrote the script for *Rocky*, tweaking every scene and line. As the script grew, he knew that if the improbable happened and this script was sold, he was the only one who could give justice to this character. He had to act in it. And so focused was he on this goal, so dedicated to his passion, that even when he was dirt poor, he still turned down offers for his screenplay. A producer offered him $125,000—more money than he'd ever had in his life—but, this producer said, Stallone couldn't act in it. So Stallone refused.

He was even offered $325,000, and Stallone (this bad a**!) still refused until they gave him the starring role. This man, with only a nickel and a button to rub together, was in NO position to play hardball. These were big-shot producers he was up against, and he said "no" time and time again. Stallone knew his worth.

He was dedicated to his passion and dream. And he took each rejection in stride to pursue his dream further.

When it was finally made in 1976, *Rocky* grossed over $200 million at the box office (Appx $1 billion dollars adjusted as of 2022). Rocky Balboa became a household name along with Stallone, whose career was from then on cemented into film history. Over fifty years later, Stallone is one of the most recognizable actors on the planet. Stallone's story teaches us that failure isn't always an external barrier we have to overcome. Sometimes the failure we have to override is settling for less than what we know at our core is worth so much more.

WALT DISNEY—A CASE STUDY

DISNEY. It's a name that's held the world's attention for nearly a century. Stallone may have Rocky, Schulz may have Charlie Brown, and Rowling may have Harry Potter, but in the realm of cultural impact, can anything beat out Walt Disney's Mickey Mouse? Just two small circles atop either side of a larger circle, it's instantly recognizable. And yet, despite its simplicity, the creation of Mickey Mouse was anything but easy.

I love Disney's story because it's chock full of both successes and failures, one always leading into the other. Even among those who know a bit about the failures he had to overcome, many don't realize that his whole life was a perfect ebb and flow of achievement and defeat. Following every peak was a valley. And while most remember Walt for his peaks, it's his foray through the valleys that makes his story that much more interesting, that much more . . . MAGICAL, as Walt might say.

Disney hailed from the east coast. His first venture into business began with Laugh-O-Gram Studios, named after a successful series of short cartoons that Disney had animated for a local theater. But in just two short years, the studio became insolvent and had to declare bankruptcy in 1923. So, having no more ties to the east coast, he packed his belongings and headed for Los Angeles, where his brother was recovering from tuberculosis. His hope was to become a cinematographer and live-action film director. With little to his name but a film reel of a short live-action production of *Alice's Adventures in Wonderland*, Walt tried selling it to every studio in town. But (what a surprise!) the City of Angels rarely hands out salvation. He was rejected by each one.

That's when a producer in New York contacted him. She was desperate for a new series and commissioned six new "Alice" shorts from Walt. This major boost of success prompted Walt and his brother, Roy, to open a studio of their own, later named "Walt Disney Studios."

The success of the Alice series brought Walt Disney Studios a new producer and a contract with Universal. But when the series came to an end, Disney felt the pressure of his new producer breathing down his neck. He wanted new material—fast. So, Disney sketched out a small black and white rabbit named Oswald, the Lucky Rabbit. Oswald became a moderate success for Universal and Walt, understandably, wanted a larger fee for the Oswald series.

The new producer saw things differently. When Disney tried to negotiate the new producer revealed that the rights to Oswald were owned by Universal. If Walt continued to stir trouble, Universal would create their own studio and produce the Oswald series on their own. Walt stuck to his guns, though, and refused to play ball. He told his animation team that they were leaving Universal, but, as if it wasn't tough enough for the poor guy, most of his team decided to stay with the producer. Walt and his brother were alone once again.

On the train ride home, Walt was dismayed but not deterred. To keep himself in a light mood, he began to sketch. What formed on the page was, unbeknownst to Walt at the time, one of the (if not the most) iconic cartoon characters in film history: Mickey Mouse.

Walt and his brother chose to bet it all and throw the dice on this character. But it was far from an instant success. Funding for a Mickey series was rejected over 300 times. And even when funding did come through, it wasn't immediately all sunshine and daisies. The series wasn't bringing in enough money, his employees were uncooperative, and Disney was pushing himself to the absolute limit. The overwhelming pressure soon crossed that limit, leading to a devastating nervous breakdown. But unlike his time at Universal, he was beholden to no one but himself. He could take some much-needed time off without the risk of losing his beloved Mickey Mouse.

Upon his return, Walt was ready to come back swinging. Not only was he ready with a new property to adapt, but he told his team they weren't going to make a short. They were going to make a full feature-length animated film with both color and sound. This had never been done before. It was known by Walt's peers as "Disney's Folly," as they were sure it would bankrupt the studio. But Disney and his team were motivated. *Snow White and The Seven Dwarfs* was released to theaters in 1937 to widespread critical acclaim, much to everyone's surprise!

The sudden surge of profit from their blockbuster hit gave the studio the confidence to invest in more feature films. But they found that recreating the success of their first feature was harder than anticipated. They released three more films, *Pinocchio, Fantasia,* and *Bambi*—all referred to as classics now!—but at the time, were considered financial failures. On top of this, World War II was in full swing. With the lack of profits, the struggles of war, and a strike brewing in his animation team, Walt was forced to make a move. He chose to diversify, and, against expert suggestions, he added televised programming to the production roster. Once again, Walt's risk-taking proved to be rewarding. Profits from *The Mickey Mouse Club* and the *Davey Crockett* miniseries flooded in, allowing Disney to fully fund an idea he'd had for years; an amusement park called Disneyland.

Now, finally, you'd think life would let up on poor Walt, right? Think again. Disneyland's opening day was rife with so many complications and setbacks that it became known as "Black Sunday." So much anticipation had been built for the park's launch that tickets sold out immediately. But this didn't stop counterfeiters from making fake tickets. More visitors than expected or planned congested the park's walkways.

The lines and wait times for rides were unbearably long, and, because this was a Los Angeles summer, the peak temperature rose over 100 degrees. Women's heels melted from the hot asphalt, the drinking fountains were out of commission due to a plumbers' strike, and many of the rides malfunctioned. But despite this, Walt continued to push forward, to override any new failure that came his way. And his legacy still ripples into the present and will continue to do so for decades to come.

Over the course of Disney's career, you can see him constantly confronted with failure. But he stood strong and met each obstacle with a brave face. He never gave up, he never quit. In fact, he might even tell you that his confrontations with failure made him less likely to quit. "All the adversity I've had in my life, all the troubles and obstacles, have strengthened me. You may not realize it when it happens, but a kick in the teeth may be the best thing in the world for you." The man learned to accept failure with success because he knew that with failure comes knowledge and with knowledge comes strength. This can be hard to do, no doubt. By definition, overriding failure isn't easy. But this is why we turn to inspirational stories for motivation and wisdom. Because if there's one thing we can take away from Disney's story, it's this: he never gave up. And if he can bounce back after every tribulation, so can you.

I'll leave you with one last quote from the GOAT, Michael Jordan: "If you quit once, it becomes a habit. Never quit!"

Chapter 8

Overriding the Unknown

It should be no surprise to you at this point that the core lesson I'm trying to impart is accepting the inevitable. Fear, sadness, anxiety—all those paralyzing emotions that seem so hard to overcome—stem from false expectations. Expecting perfection in your endeavors will bring you nothing but misery. Failure should not only be expected but anticipated. It's an inevitable consequence of life, so why screw yourself over by not preparing for it? Anticipate and be ready.

But even more so than failure, the true inevitability that we all must face is the Unknown. At no point in your life are you going to have it all figured out. You're never going to know the exact, proper steps to take, what the future will hold, or even how much effort you'll have to give to achieve your goals. It's inevitable not to know, and it's natural. But it's also natural to be fearful of the unknown. So don't go kicking yourself into high gear, thinking yourself courageous. The point isn't to get rid of the fear; it's to approach it in the best way possible. And the answer is actually a topic we've already briefly touched on: the trait of Open-Mindedness.

If you recall, I described open-mindedness in the context of opening yourself up to opportunity and conversation. Openness is merely the act of admitting to yourself that your preconceptions or expectations of the world are lacking. In other words, openness is accepting that you do not know everything. Now, I understand that this may be easier said than done. But let's take a look at the logic of it through the concept of doubling down.

The thought process behind openness goes something like this: "everything happens for a reason." I know, I know, it's a cliche saying. But it's more than just a mindless truism. Within it is the primary tool for achieving openness. See, think of it in terms of Blackjack and doubling down. The longer you play the game and when multiple failures happen in a row, the bigger the bets have to be. So further down the line, when that sweet "21" slides in front of you, you'll walk away far more ahead. Blackjack came at the right time. And more often than not, the big wins happen to those who have learned from their previous failures and put everything they had into their successes…and the ones that keep stepping up to the table. You may not know when you're going to beat the dealer in life, but regardless, each experience is either a lesson or a win. Each experience happened for a reason. It just might be that the reason for all the prior failures was a much-needed lesson so that you could win big once the Blackjack hit.

For those of you who still may be raising an eyebrow at this concept (maybe you're a bit more mathematically minded), let's take a look at the math of Blackjack that we discussed in a previous chapter. To get the basics out of the way, Blackjack is when you're dealt an ace and a face card—that sweet "21." This is an automatic win unless the dealer matches your hand. But a Blackjack win is more important than your normal, run-of-the-mill win because winning with a Blackjack gets you a greater payback than a regular bet. To reiterate the math behind this, some tables pay 6/5 while others pay as much as 3/2. So, let's say you've just bet $100. Typically, a win will get you a $100 profit. But a Blackjack win pays what you put in PLUS 50 percent on a 3/2 table. That $100 bet with a Blackjack win just returned $150!

When we take a look at this example and we recontextualize it, the beauty of openness should reveal itself. Look at it like this. I've been talking about negative progression, about doubling the bet (i.e., doubling your effort) so that you come out one step ahead. But guess what? Sometimes things go so perfectly, sometimes the stars align just right that you're not just one step ahead, but one step ahead plus 50 percent! I don't think I have to say it . . . but when that happens, you're absolutely killing it! So, to elaborate, if you feel daunted and find yourself saying, "Well, sh*t, I put it in all this effort and only got what I put in," don't fret. Know that sometimes . . . sometimes, you hit a Blackjack, and you'll realize that every failure, and every minor win, happened for a reason. To take the gambling analogy out of this, it's saying that although you may just be improving one step at a time, back and forth with wins and losses, eventually, to those that keep putting themselves out there, keep pushing, keep trying… eventually there will be massive wins.

But if this is still too conceptual, let me extend an olive branch. Let's look at an example of these ideas working in the real world.

RING DOORBELLS CASE STUDY

In 2013, thirty-seven-year-old inventor, Jamie Siminoff, pitched his new invention to the investors on the television show, Shark Tank. He tried as best he could to get one of them to invest in his product but was ultimately rejected by every shark. He left, to his dismay, without a deal. But in five short years, Siminoff, overriding this failure and the unknown, would turn that failure into something much, much greater.

When he originally pitched his product to the sharks, his product was called Doorbot. It sold a Wi-Fi enabled doorbell that allowed users to see and communicate with people as they arrived at the front door. The only shark who was interested in funding this product was Kevin O'Leary. But O'Leary made an offer that Siminoff considered unacceptable. So . . . he left empty-handed.

Siminoff told CNBC Make It, "I remember after that 'Shark Tank' episode literally being in tears. I needed the money. We were out of money at the time."

He'd sunk $10,000 into building props for the pitch. And the company—a small staff of eight people—had spent a month preparing for the show. Leaving with no investment felt to Siminoff as if all that effort and money had been a complete waste, just money down the drain.

And it wasn't just the money that cut down Siminoff's spirit. The critiques from big-time investors like Mark Cuban and Lori Greiner about Doorbot's salability were objections he'd continue to hear. "I can't count the number of people who didn't invest in this, who said 'no,' the number of people who said it was going to fail," Siminoff said. "I don't think Excel could hold the number of records for it."

I'm sure these doubts infected Siminoff's mind. The unknown must've been creeping in. What does he do next? Is this product worth it? "Should I double down and keep pouring money into this product no one believes in?"

Luckily for Siminoff, he chose to do just that.

Though the sharks didn't invest, Siminoff slowly began to see the reputation of his product grow. The episode had garnered so much publicity for the company that it soon catapulted out of its financial woes. In just five years' time, in 2018, Siminoff sold his company (now called "Ring") to Amazon for one billion dollars. Yes, that's right. Billion. With a "B."

The unknown haunted him, sure, but he held out and overrode it. He doubled down, and, in the process, kept an eye out for opportunities. By keeping himself open and prepared, he won far more than he had put in. This is the attitude that you should inhabit when confronted with the unknown. Realize that, even in the face of the unknown, everything happens for a reason and a Blackjack comes in due time, as long as you keep your eyes open.

This is a lesson I struggled to learn and incorporate into my own daily life. It's a difficult lesson, I understand. When life smacks you in the face and no pathway seems correct, feelings of anxiety can be hard to overcome. But being open, and remaining teachable at all times, has been a guarantee of success in my life. In fact, let me just show you.

Openness to timing and opportunity, overriding the unknown—I can, personally, attribute my largest success as a direct result of this mindset. I described earlier my first large business failure in my company called "Pridetagz." It was a major blow to my pride, my self-confidence, and also my wallet. I was over $100k in debt, but I didn't let this stop me.

I moved forward to my next business venture with not much more than the lessons I'd learned. This business was called Identity Partners, a small experiential marketing agency with very few clients . . . which also failed. But this time around, I didn't just lose money, I also lost a friendship with my business partner where our relationship turned so sour that a lawsuit ensued. I was now over $100k in debt and on the cusp of a lawsuit with a former close friend. But I kept going, striving forward in the hope that success would stick. I kept my mind open to the next opportunity.

And when it came, I started up my third business. It was similar to Identity Partners, but it was now simply Identity Marketing. With no partner to assist me, I planned for this company to be an experiential STAFFING agency. I wasn't sure if the third time was going to be effective. I'd had far fewer resources than my first two attempts. But I knew deep down that the right time would come if I only kept my eyes open and the lessons I'd learned in mind.

In eighteen months, Identity Marketing went from zero to seven figures in revenue, and has been a million-dollar revenue business, year over year, for almost a decade!

What changed? Why was this business successful?

Of course, I couldn't have known that the third time was going to be the Blackjack win I'd been hoping for. My track record certainly left a lot to be desired. But with each failure, I doubled my efforts by using the lessons I'd picked up from the previous failure. I didn't know if the lessons would be enough to sustain a successful business. But what I did know was this: if I kept my mind open to every teachable moment, the doubling of my efforts would eventually be met with a Blackjack win.

To give you the basic rundown, my first business was collegiate dog tags. I received a decently sized bank start-up loan of about $100k. After I got collegiate licensing, I figured the company would run smooth as butter. Except . . . I only had one actual product. So, when the recession hit, it hit my company twice as hard. With only one product to keep the business afloat, I was dead in the water. I took several, "Hail Mary," shots in a desperate attempt to rise above the poor economic climate, but all I managed to do was burn through my capital. The issue was that I didn't know how to properly manage a budget runway. Soon enough, I ran out of money. But now I had a massive debt to pay off on top of the bills. So back I went to my "day job" of managing promotional events. UGH.

But the fires of passion weren't completely snuffed out. I knew what the issues were with the previous business, and I knew that when the next opportunity arrived, I'd be ready.

When it did arrive, it was the chance to start Identity Partners with my good friend, who, at one point, had been my boss. We were going to start our own "boutique," experiential marketing agency. On paper, we didn't have any confirmed clients, but we did know a few potential companies we could work with, like the NCAA and (potentially) Coca-Cola. My good friend and business partner had some great connections over at Coca-Cola, and we had some fan fest work already lined up with the NCAA. Once again, everything was looking great.

But ultimately, these connections led to a dead end. Our company had been up and running for less than a year and we were already running out of options. Our revenue stream was, frankly, crap, and all we had left to prove ourselves was the chance to staff some events in the field. Ironically, the companies we were trying to compete against were the agencies that could (and should) have been our clients. We had an excellent reputation in the experiential world, but we were now trying going straight to brand. It didn't make sense for us to compete against agencies that were $20–50M companies.

But they respected the work we'd done for them in the past, so, in 2010–2011, they gave us our final opportunity to staff some events. I said we'd do whatever work they could give us. They gave us the 2011 Superbowl played in Dallas, TX. Sounds good, no? Well, we went from staffing one to two events of four to six people for a single day to 80–120 people for ten straight days. I'll go slightly more into detail on this in the next chapter.

Long story short, I made it work. This was my client, my event to staff and manage, and nothing was going to stop me from nailing this opportunity. I pulled out all the stops and made it happen. During the entire endeavor, I held the lessons from my previous failure to fuel my effort while always keeping an eye out for potential new lessons. It's true, I didn't know if I'd be able to pull it off. And how the h*ll did I know how to scale up to this extent!? I didn't know . . . but whatever happened, I knew there'd be something to be gained, whether it'd be a Blackjack win or a lesson.

Fortunately, I did manage to "win" the event. But unfortunately, this was the beginning of the end of my friendship. My business partner and I began to have long arguments on the importance of fast communication with clients. This soon led to more general disagreements about each other's availability in a fast-paced industry that doesn't "take personal time." Without getting too deep into it, I believe he just wasn't cut out to be an entrepreneur. It didn't mean enough to him.

I won't lie. It hurt. But because I'd maintained an open mind, I'd picked up another lesson. Best friends don't make the best business partners. So, after avoiding the ugly part of a lawsuit, I decided to start another company, Identity Marketing. I once again was facing the unknown. But doubling down had gotten me that much closer to a Blackjack win, so I had a strong feeling I would be seeing that ace and face card soon enough. I chose to streamline the company's services and, as they were my bread and butter, stuck strictly to staffing events. Within a couple months, we'd done over $100k in revenue, and in just eighteen months, we'd reached $1M.

From that point forward, I was off to the races. Now I knew how to operate lean and without capital; I knew who to partner with and who to avoid; I knew when to spot and how to seize the best opportunities. I learned how to understand who is better suited to be clients and how to parlay a solid reputation into hundreds of thousands of dollars earned every year. My Blackjack win was here. Again, I'll provide a few more details on this instance in the next chapter.

So, to bring this back to overriding the unknown, we can look at my first failure with Pridetagz. I couldn't have been in a more vulnerable position than that. I'd been as green as they come in terms of running my own business, and my lack of preparation was tested when the recession hit. But, having kept my mind open, the unknown wasn't as frightening. Doubling my efforts came easier when the lessons I'd learned had filled in the gaps in my knowledge.

And the same process occurred when the cracks of Identity Partners started to show. I didn't know if it was going to succeed, but I kept myself teachable and ready to learn. I then combined all the lessons to double down once again, without any capital and a huge debt. With this openness to learn, some good timing, good luck, and a lot of hard work, I'd say I got the Blackjack I'd been looking for. I was more than just one step ahead from where I'd started. I was finally on the fast track.

But, after giving my personal example, I'm sure the real question in your mind is, "How does this translate to my life?" You may have a good grasp of the importance of an open mindset, but I want to emphasize that this works in all aspects of life. You're going to fail in relationships, marriages, daily activities like cooking, cleaning, raising kids, sports, work, sales, friendships. And in each new venture, you're going to have to face the unknown, which is inevitable and understandably discomforting. But if you can override failure, you can override the unknown. With every failure comes a lesson. The key is in keeping your mind and eyes open to new possibilities, new opportunities, to new lessons. You should be constantly taking mental notes of what works and what doesn't so that when your next adventure begins, you'll have the necessary tools to double your effort with confidence.

Think of it like a boy's first experience in the dating world. What's the typical story we all know? He asks out this girl and gets rejected. Perhaps because he didn't have enough self-confidence or didn't work hard enough to make himself attractive. It could be any number of reasons. So, he works on himself ever so slightly and asks out another. Only this time, he gets the go-ahead. The date begins and he discovers he shares nothing in common with this girl. (In fact, sometimes he realizes he doesn't even really like being around her!) It's back to the proverbial drawing board.

But now he's a little closer to knowing what he wants. He knows that he needs to find someone he's compatible with. He then comes across a girl who's got a similar taste in music. Still, he doesn't know if this relationship will last, but his passion is enough to give it a go. But, of course, he learns that a shared taste in music isn't enough to sustain a relationship. And the cycle continues. The trick, though, is keeping your mind open to the lessons each failed relationship provided. These could be flaws with compatibility or personal flaws that you need to work out on your own. We're not saints. There's almost always something that can be fixed within us. You just have to be ready and open enough to see those flaws when you inevitably face them.

Ultimately, overriding ignorance involves self-responsibility. You have to be brave enough to be honest with yourself. And this can only be done through openness, which, if taken on valiantly, will lead you to that perfect someone, your forever person. I guarantee you, too, that when that happens, they will have arrived at just the right time.

This also applies to landing your dream job. You only land your dream job after cycling through different jobs that were, to you, merely a paycheck. I'm sure we've all been in a situation in which we've taken a job, believing full well that a long-lasting career will come from it. Only then to realize, after a year or two of service, that this job came with a load of baggage that isn't worth your blood, sweat, and tears. Maybe the hours are too long. Maybe the boss doesn't respect you. Maybe the company continues to bring outside hires, preventing you from climbing the ladder. Or perhaps it's the industry as a whole! Your initial field of choice wasn't as fulfilling as you once thought it was. Like my former friend and business partner. He and I both discovered that he wasn't cut out to be an entrepreneur at that point in his life. It required much more than he was willing to give.

This is a common occurrence, guys! It's okay to be unsure of where you're at. But like the young boy's first dating experience, you wouldn't give him the advice to quit dating when he feels those first seeds of doubt. No! Of course not! You'd tell him to buck up. Get back in the game! Learn from what didn't work and find the partner of your dreams. In the same vein, fear of the unknown shouldn't stop you from finding your dream job. It may seem scary, but when you're armed with an open attitude, you've got little to lose and only lessons to gain.

If you remain teachable, remain open, then you'll find what you will and won't put up with in a career. You'll know the industry that you not only excel at but are also excited to be a part of. Just like your forever person, you'll land your dream job—and at just the right time.

Before we hop into the next chapter, I'll leave you with one last example. Let's say you're working on closing a client. But due to this or that circumstance, the deal isn't closed, and you miss out on the client's business. You may have lost their business, but you learned something about communication with this person. You realize that you made some mistakes that could be remedied.

So, then your next potential client comes into your crosshairs. You do your best to fix your previous mistakes, but something's still off. Perhaps you weren't competitive enough on price, but now you know it was nothing you did specifically. On your third potential sale, you double down again, gathering up all the lessons you've learned. But you discover they're just not the right person/company for your services. You may have wasted your time on the wrong person, sure. Look at what you gained though. You now have a better idea of your ideal clientele.

Now it's your fourth attempt. And here is where you get lucky. Turns out this fourth client is bidding out a contract ten times the size of the first three clients. And because you've kept an open attitude, you approach the unknown landscape with confidence. You use your communication lessons, you have your pricing just right, and you're able to pin this client down as your ideal fit. You've done everything right. What have you got to show for it? Well, you didn't just land a sale; you got a MONSTER. Or what I like to call . . . BLACKJACK.

Chapter 9

Mental Fortitude—
The Ultimate Mental Override

f I am going to consider myself a failure expert, I'm pretty
sure I should prove my own experience of failures, how they
left me temporarily broken and realizing the only thing I
can't get back from these situations of desperation and failure
is the most valuable commodity of them all: time. Fortunately, I
get to speak from experience to let you not feel so alone.

I have a quote that I have said on several occasions after
I used it as a mantra in my first business when things weren't
going well. It started actually when I was giving advice to someone going through the same struggles starting their business as
I was. I told him, just remember one thing, it's not the mornings

you wake up and everything is going well that define who we are, it's the mornings we wake up, and despite everything going wrong, feeling like the world is against us and we don't want to get out of bed but we do and we get to work anyways . . . that truly defines us. This is MENTAL FORTITUDE.

As I have progressed as an entrepreneur, speaker, and coach I have gotten to hear other people's heart wrenching stories of despair and I've gotten a solid taste of my own. Through Covid we have gotten to see many people's lives completely implode, meanwhile we've seen other's businesses explode. Look no further than one of the greatest speakers and thought leaders of all time, Tony Robbins, for this message.

At the beginning of the COVID-19 pandemic Tony Robbins had one of his flagship programs "Unleash the Power Within" conferences planned that was set to have tens of thousands of people in attendance in person. This conference was planned to be in California, and we know how swift their shut down was. Tony had to think creatively, and he decided to move the event on short notice to Las Vegas, because God knows, Vegas would have never been shut down. News flash, and if you have been living in a shanty in Idaho, Vegas just like the rest of the country was shut down as well.

His team flirted with the idea of moving virtual and this felt like an impossibility and the end of the world for Tony. But, after some discussion they decided if they were going to do it, they had to go big and do it right. It destroyed Tony that his life blood was essentially being cancelled by this illness. This was a common feeling to many of us all over the world. I personally have had a career in events for the last fifteen-plus years, so I understand this to my core. Tony just happened to handle it better than most, AND he found an amazing silver lining.

He swallowed his preconceived notions of what virtual looked like in the past and he gave it a chance. It turned out to be a complete GAME CHANGER. Over the last couple years, it has allowed hundreds of thousands of people to get to see this event, and other Tony Robbins style events, who wouldn't have had the opportunity to travel or experience it. Tony is getting to reach more people and fulfill his destiny and dream to touch millions of people's lives. What's great is that he is giving the opportunity for families, groups of friends, stay-at-home moms and others the opportunity to hear a life-changing message that wouldn't have been able to in the past. This allowed him to have more impact on a personal level and allowed him to expand his revenue exponentially.

In summary . . . using Tony's favorite saying, "Life doesn't happen to you, it happens FOR you." It gives you the opportunity to mobilize your life and find the path that you may have never seen in the past, but the key is to search for that silver lining and new opportunities. This goes the same for the failures that seemingly crush us. Take a step back and start to think about where you can go from here.

I don't know if anyone has watched *This Is Us* . . . personally I loved the show, can't get enough. It has a such a variety of cast that every episode manages to perfectly manipulate the audience into being emotionally connected to one character at different points . . . anyway . . . not the point here. Back to my point . . . In the beginning of the fourth season there is a bit, and I won't giveaway the character or the full story but there is an anecdote to life that fits here perfectly.

There is a character introduced who is a blind musician. This character, although blind, appears to be very self-sufficient and is in the process of making breakfast when his service dog accidentally knocks over the plate with his meal. Something that of course would frustrate and annoy even a sighted person. He handled it in stride however, and instead of making a new meal he ends up going to a diner to get breakfast. At this breakfast he ends up meeting a waitress that he hits it off with.

It was alluded to in the show that, prior to this chance encounter, the blind musician was abusing alcohol, depressed, and afraid his career was going nowhere, and in this moment, he meets what it turns out to be his future wife, and the songs he writes about their life together elevates his career. Later in the show when they are in their home, there is a framed broken plate on the wall. This is a perfect reminder that even in the moments when everything seems to be going wrong and you are at the end of your rope that a positive perspective on life will allow you to realize that something amazing can and will come out of it. Again, life is happening FOR you, not to you.

I understand this is a TV show, so I'd like to get back into reality, my reality in fact. I'll go over a personal story regarding how I got to where I am now in my speaking and coaching career. Hell, how I got to where I am writing this book right now. My experience in the stock market and the failures from this led me directly to this book.

In 2018, I got into options trading in the stock market. I took some inexpensive classes and did a lot of my own research on how it worked and how to invest. For those of you that don't understand options, I'll make this as simple as possible. For a premium you get to hold 100 shares of stock you probably wouldn't buy otherwise. It sounds great on paper but the volatility of this kind of investing is immense. You can play slow, steady and smart, which is how I began but as I started to get more comfortable, I became an options gunslinger, trying to trade $50k+ worth of volatile options from my telephone . . . yes, I know, dumb idea.

However, in these several months of options trading I was consistently learning lessons from my mistakes. The great thing is I rarely made the same mistake twice, but that didn't mean I didn't incur massive losses.

After losing thousands of dollars in the stock market, specifically my last major "bad" options mistake that was a 7k in one hour mistake, I looked at this string of negative events as a message from the universe. It was time to think about what the h*ll I was doing. I still talk to people today about how big a mistake I made that year in the stock market and at moments I feel a little salty, and then in that exact moment I quickly realize that everything I do today and who I have become is because of those moments, and the failures that came before it.

If I had made money on these trades the opposite way and I kept pressing and kept pressing I could still be doing something I wasn't destined to do, and wouldn't be fulfilling my duty to help people, to make the world better. Or I could have kept pressing and maybe I would have doubled down again and gone even further and ended up putting a higher amount of money in the mix and lost everything. Or maybe, I'd lose enough where I decided to do the same thing that I'm doing now but a year later, two years later, five years later who knows. The fact is, time is the one commodity that is irreplaceable, and I would not have wanted to waste any more time not doing what I love, which is talking to audiences, talking to business' and writing a book like you are reading right now.

I want to touch a little more on some of the stories and anecdotes from earlier chapters to put them more into context.

I want to go back a bit in time to my promotional staffing agency that I ran for almost a decade that was met with success more often than not. However, there were a few major failures and moments of despair that I want to bring up. I had a successful, seven-figure revenue business, year after year, but at one point I was looking at adding one million dollars of revenue based on two upcoming clients. One client was a woman who would hire me to staff international events with a contracted team, all over the world, and that would be approximately $400k of new business. The other was a client whose represented brand was Columbia launching their Omni Heat brand of clothes, that should have been another 750k in business based on original scope of work.

All in a matter of four hours, after working on these clients over a span of three months I came to find out I lost both clients in the blink of an eye. The international client was painful for many reasons, but the worst was that I had hired a good friend of mine who ended up leaving her job in Chicago and moving to Dallas to take this job as the main planner. The day she arrived in Dallas was when, suddenly, the client went dark—not returning calls, emails, texts—out of nowhere. My friend was set to go to her office almost immediately upon her move. So, at about 1 p.m. on this day of ultimate failure, I realized that the client had sold her business in the middle of the night a few nights prior, and the gig was gone, she was gone, and the business was gone. I was devastated not just because of the loss of business, but because I felt I hurt my close friend as I didn't have work for her, and I felt as though I had screwed her over.

Fun fact, I have still never spoken to that business owner, she never had the decency to reach out and just talk with me like an adult. This one hurt but in the end, it worked out for all of us as my friend needed to leave her job anyways and ended up going to back to Chicago to take a different job that led to her meeting her now husband where they have an amazing life, amazing home and blessed life. May not have happened that way without this "life tangent" she had to take. With that said . . . DON'T EVER BE THAT WOMAN that doesn't call and has a conversation with someone you just screwed over.

Now, let's fast forward a whopping five hours. I had been working with this one client since they won the bid to do the Columbia work. I actually wrote the staffing portion of their deck, and they "celebrated with me" when they won the bid. I was told it was my business, period, point blank. Based on our previous work on this brand and similar events I was given the scope of work and I returned a simple quote. The account manager was switched midway through the process and that's where the problems began.

As the weeks went by after the first estimate, I provided revision after revision based on their pricing request, asking for lower and lower pay for staff, cutting my mark-ups. But I still found where my company could profit as I lowered the esti-mate all the way down from over $700k to $412k, and I'll never forget that number. I shaved over $300k off the quote against the best interests of my company and the program. As I slowly came down it became harder and harder to get ahold of the account director, and this gave me some concern, but there was never a mention that I was bidding against anyone, as that wasn't ever mentioned as I was told from day one, this was my business.

Now, it's about 6 p.m. at night and I decided to throw up a Hail Mary and call after hours to see if I can get a hold of the account director. She accidentally picked up, not knowing it would be me, and there was no one there to screen my call. At this moment, on the same day that I lost the other business, I was informed that she decided to go in another direction with another company that came in right at 400k, which was the number she wanted. Mind you she told them the number she wanted, never told that to me. After all of that I needed to come in 12k lower, and I would have matched this other company.

So, there it was, almost a million dollars in one day, an amount of business that would have changed my bottom line drastically. I turned white. I felt as though the wind had com-pletely been knocked out of me and all the air had left my body. I really was in a place of complete despair with a feeling of utter and complete sadness. For a couple days, I sulked so badly that I didn't get off the couch. I was that guy that just sat there with a blanket on the couch and watched crappy TV shows on repeat. I didn't want to move. I felt that not only that I had failed, but that I had also been a fraud to everyone I had given business advice to over the last few years. People looked up to my expertise and at the time, not understanding the power of failure, this completely destroyed me. I remember breaking down and crying a couple times because I really felt like I lost my identity as a "winner."

It was like I completely forgot that I still had a million-dollar business that I had started from the ground up, with no capital and still had plenty of clients and a great business. It took a couple weeks to get out of this funk, where I had no energy, no motivation and no drive. Then all of a sudden, just like a bad break up, I started to come out of it, and a couple months later I even got to see the silver lining.

That year, about a month and a half later when the program was set to start, my father passed away. This just so happened to be the second or third week of the program and with what I was going through it would have been incredibly difficult to balance the two things in my life. ESPECIALLY since I would have sacrificed the quality of staff to the whim of the account manager trying to cut corners. Right as my father passed away, I was getting calls from this client for help because the company that did undercut was FAILING MISERABLY because they didn't have the caliber of staff their client wanted.

We ended up staffing a small portion of their events along the way in order to help this program. So ultimately, we never would have had a successful program and it would have been insanely taxing along the way with everything going on in my personal life. Also, because of our ability to assist this program when things were rocky, we also solidified more future business with this company because of our hard work in saving parts of the program. In the end, it did indeed work out.

Through this failure, the one thing I learned is that the most valuable commodity is time, something we can't get back, and in the future these "setbacks," are just that, setbacks and that when big failures happen I will be prepared, I'll take a moment to step back and assess, look for the benefits of any missteps and move forward as fast as possible.

Now, I'm going to go back even further to my first foray into the world of entrepreneurialism. My first business was a company I founded called "Pridetagz." It was a business based on military style dog tags with different branding on them and collegiate logos. The concept was to have something that showed you were a part of something bigger than yourself, and with that you'd wear the necklace to show your fandom or the part of being part of a bigger community.

I managed to secure a six-figure loan from a bank with minimal collateral based on a pretty killer business plan, if I may say so myself. This business started in 2007, I know . . . good timing. After achieving several collegiate licenses, I achieved what should have been a pretty legit start up product. Any collegiate licensed items at this time were boasting very solid early valuations, however as you all know, 2008 put a massive halt to most "extra spending," Immediately the college market shifted, and my business prospects dried up and my $100k+ loan was quickly looking very difficult to pay back and the business was struggling.

I was almost out of money from the loan and the business was failing. I didn't hit rock bottom just yet, but it was coming. Using some of my old contacts from living in Milwaukee I threw up a Hail Mary to get licensing for Harley Davidsons'

105-year anniversary celebration coming up. I felt as though I could get licensing on these Harley dog tags based on my relationships that worked for Harley. I was verbally told it would be no problem so I started producing thousands of these dog tags with the last bit of my financial resources hoping this would set me up for some success. With a month left leading up to the celebration and with a million bikes descending on Milwaukee, I was told another company snatched up ALL licensing for metal objects and I was SOL with a bunch of illegally produced merchandise.

It gets worse. Since I could not sell these items to any stores that were selling commemorative items, it left me with one option. I began to sell them in bars and on street corners. I was able to get my friends and even my mother to help hock these with me. I, for all intents and purposes, had become a street hustler, selling illegal jewelry on street corners in Milwaukee. I felt like a complete failure. It was one of the only mental breakdowns or panic attacks I've ever had in my life. I still remember sitting in my car after my first day out there, after selling three pairs of dog tags, and thinking this was the end of the world. I remember talking to my mom on the phone in a complete shambles. To this day, I have made it a mission to make sure I never put myself in that position again, to never feel the way I felt that night. Thankfully, I was able to learn from the mistakes to ensure I would not have to sell items on a street corner ever again.

With that said, there were massive silver linings that I didn't see at the time because I was, of course, too close to the situation. I couldn't step back and look at a bigger picture. It felt like the end of the world as I'm sure you could imagine.

It was clear to me at that moment that not only did I fail, but I was also a failure.

Fortunately, with the help of my friends, some local bars, and my mom coming into town to save the day, I at least broke even on my initial spend. Not the $20k I was hoping for, but it could have been a lot worse. I still remember the main bar that allowed me to use their location to let me sell tags out of their location and even sell them from the bar giving me the cash they made, and how much that meant to me. I came back years later when I had a successful business and tipped the bar owner, who was also a bartender, $100 and told them how much that act of kindness meant to me. It gave me faith that things could have been much worse.

The silver linings don't stop here. I found out some other things going on with my mother, that I didn't know until a couple years later. It turns out, the recession, along with some injuries my mom had sustained, caused her to lose her chiropractic business. She was in massive debt, had lost her business and was all but broken. Her coming to Milwaukee to help me was going to be her goodbye to me. She had been battling massive depression and this was slated to be her "last hurrah." She was planning on committing suicide when she returned home.

What kept her alive was her seeing me struggling. It gave her purpose; it showed her that her son still needed her. Her mission as a mother was not complete, my failure had kept my mom alive. What if I was achieving a mild level of success? What if I didn't need her anymore at this point? I may not have felt like a failure in that moment, but I would have lost my mom. It's so important to take a step back and realize sometimes life gives you what you need and not what you want. This was such a powerful lesson I learned from this failure that is still with me today.

My second business was an experiential marketing agency that I started with a close friend of mine when I moved to Dallas, Texas. He had years of experience in this world working for the company where he and I met, and where he was originally my manager. He was under the impression that he had many clients that would follow and that we'd have a booming business right when we got started, including having a huge client in Coca-Cola. Spoiler Alert that client never materialized.

To sum up this business, we managed to take on a few very small events and it turns out his relationships and reputation in the industry weren't exactly as presented. He was well liked but had made some pretty huge mistakes in recent years that had affected our credibility and hampered our ability to get clients. Worse yet, I learned that the good reputation we had was with the marketing agencies, like ours, and not with the brands. Those agencies were now our competition and were much larger and with better resources.

After we struggled for several months, I was presented with a proposition while doing contract work for another gig and I seized the opportunity. The staffing agency that was to provide brand ambassadors was at 50 percent capacity and just like that the next ideation of this business was formed. I was asked if my young agency could do staffing of promotional models and brand ambassadors. I said yes, and to the dismay of my close friend and business partner he said that was not the business we were in. I can tell you at that point we were in the business of whatever we could make money from, and this was very close to the world we were already in, but not finding any success. It was a very logical pivot, and it would end up leading me to the path of a million dollar a year revenue company.

We took on a small event for the World Series in Texas and found a way to make it happen with around six total staff requested. That was our test, and the reward was the opportunity to staff the Superbowl for *Sports Illustrated*, Bing and Pepsi for this major agency in Dallas, TX. This would entail multiple locations and some days almost 100 total staff. Yes . . . six to then 100, and on top of that the Superbowl is one of the hardest events to staff because it requires credentialling of staff a few months in advance, so you have to lock people in early and hope they block these ten days off in their calendar.

I'll add to the level of difficulty and tell you at the time there were MINIMAL resources to find staff in comparison to today. There was Craigs list and friends of friends, that was about it, for a company that didn't already have a built-in roster. It was also a very complicated schedule and since this was my client, and my business partner was often unavailable around holidays, I took the helm on the staffing process. Once I started, however, it was very difficult to hand anything over, so I ended up staffing the whole thing.

Fast forward to the Superbowl that year in Dallas . . . Ice storms the week leading up, and BAD ONES. We had insanely cold temperatures in the area, which made some of the outdoor activities very difficult for the staff. We had to replace, on some days, 20 percent of our staff because of inability to drive, getting in accidents and other unforeseen issues. Mind you, as I stated earlier, we had to have everyone working credentialled months in advance and with, depending on the day losing twenty people this because insanely difficult and I was shooting from the hip on getting replacements. This was, to this date, the hardest week of my life, bar none.

In the end, I made it happen and it began the rift in the partnership that only got worse over time. We made decent money with this event that, although it was all my work, we split based on our ownership percentage, which was my 45 percent to his 55 percent. even though this doubled the company's lifetime revenue in one ten-day segment. Either way, my issue wasn't in the split, it was in the lack of partnership. As time wore on our relationship grew more strained as he didn't understand what it takes to be a founder, which means living in your job, and sacrificing personal time. This isn't forever, but it is part of the start-up process, way more often than not.

The proverbial sh*t hit the fan later that year when we decided to part ways leading into a weekend to which I thought was amicable, but unfortunately woke up with the bank account frozen by him and my email locked out (even though I was in the process of continuing business), because that's what I was always doing, and you have to do especially since it was my client. Needless to say, things got ugly for a couple weeks and out of it I had to file a lawsuit and settle out of court to get my money back; I had to start over from this business and lost one of my best friends in the process.

At that point, although being super close this is when I found out many things about my business partner including some of his personal wrongdoings and issues which led me to realize he definitely had some "pathological liar" tendencies. Our total revenue in the year and a half we were in business was less than $250k, yet he told people that he had brough in 1.2 million dollars in business and I had no reason to not want to continue doing business with him. This illustrates my pathological liar comment from a second ago.

So here I was, back to square one, starting over, taking my one client with me and rebranding the company. Fast forward just seventeen months from this point, with absolutely no capital except one client who paid on a net 30 (paid invoice within thirty days of receipt). I was able to reach 1 million dollars in revenue, and then reached one million every year thereafter for the greater part of a decade.

So, taking these two failures into consideration, I realize how important these failures were to me, leading to the success of this business. I learned so many things in these few instances. I learned from Pridetagz that timing means everything, and don't jump the gun until you have something signed on the dotted line. I learned the importance of spending money wisely, and I learned how to be flexible. I also learned that sometimes, with a positive mindset there is a silver lining to failure, as I mentioned with what happened with my mother.

In the marketing agency I also learned the importance of knowing your niche. I learned that sometimes you have to trust your gut, best friend or not, and I learned that sometimes a pivot can make a world of difference. I also found out that sometimes, if you can find a way to succeed in the hardest of situations, like what happened to us during the Superbowl, with the ice storms and weather, then if you can find a way to succeed despite all odds, things will get easier. This goes back to one of my favorite

Les Brown quotes. If you do what is easy, life will be hard, and if you do what is hard, life will be easy.

So how do you become strong in mind? You treat your mind like a muscle, and you feed it positivity and positive messages. First off... actively take action when you find your mind spiraling and tell yourself to stop, I'm not kidding, say it out loud.

Chapter 10

Course Correct—
The Ultimate Set-Up

We have covered a myriad of different tips, tricks, anecdotes, recipes and more that change one's mindset to see a completely different way to look at life, success and ultimately the journey.

This is where we take everything we've talked about, take a second to collect ourselves and make sure we are on the right course. This is also where we course-correct and decide what our future holds. Where are you going to place your time and energy, so it best serves you to not only reach success, but happiness as well.

We need to make sure we correct our course to marry happiness and success into one thought instead of opposing forces. This sounds easy, but it's often the most disconnected ideology we have in our society.

Often some of the most depressed people, and those prone to high rates of suicide, are also those with large bank accounts, high levels of career success, and appearances on social media that everything is perfect. You can create the life of your dreams but if you haven't embraced how to handle the bumps in the road, or to recognize the moments you should enjoy and feel joy for (the little things), then this amazing life will feel empty.

We have to learn to fill our cup with the journey, not with just the victories . . . call it cheesy, call it overused, but sometimes the most simple thoughts are the way to completely change mindset. Some people say the most successful people in this world believe one line more than anything else, and it's simply that, "everything happens for a reason." I'm going to say that is one way to merge success and happiness. In the end, even in failure, this mindset tells you that with a positive attitude you are able to find joy when things go wrong.

I have a very quick personal story to go along with this, and that goes along with the overriding mindset that you never know when the universe or God has a plan, and has a reason for when things go wrong. Last year my Girlfriend had just gotten a new (used) horse trailer that she had been driving that was well over 10k pounds empty. Soon after the purchase there were some things that went wrong and needed an immediate fix. At the end of the day, this had a cost several thousand dollars. Ordinarily this is a moment where we get frustrated, and angry for incurred expenses that we didn't expect, but in the end there might be a positive way to look at it.

One night, late after a rodeo, Kelly was driving a borrowed truck and a loaner trailer about a mile ahead of me, because her big, heavy one was in the shop. She came around a corner on a small country road. There had been a very bad accident that had happened, and the extra police there didn't think about the need to warn people coming around the curve.

When she drove around the curve at 65 miles per hour, she immediately slammed on the brakes and was able to stop in time before crashing into the car in front of her. If she had had an extra 5–7k of weight behind her, that would have caused an extra thirty to forty feet MINIMUM to stop. This could have been incredibly ugly; she could have plowed through the cars, hurt others, she could have twisted and jackknifed off the road and hurt herself or her horses. So many different things could have happened, and her only saving grace was the lighter trailer.

Think about this reference next time things take a turn you don't want to see. You have no idea how the bad things happening might be for a greater purpose. Often you will not see them as clearly as something like this, but you simply never know how that timing can change an outcome. To be clear, we are human and we are allowed to get upset when something goes wrong, or there is an unforeseen bill, breakdown, needed fix, etc. But the key is taking a breath and realizing, "everything happens for a reason."

The sooner we can shift our mindset to that, let's look at the bigger picture, or think of one of Tony Robbins' go-to phrases,

"Life happens for us, not to us." Then you have shifted your mindset to something that changes every element of your life.

So, now that we've talked about changing the outlook on the negatives, how do we embrace the positive so that we enjoy those feelings enough to be happy? First off, the moment of success is NOT the only moments we should find joy in. This is where the concept of peace and gratitude come into play. Observe everything around you, and find gratitude in these items. If you are a negative person with issues with depression that other people would look at you and your life and say I don't get it . . . then this is for you.

START A GRATITUDE JOURNAL TODAY. You have to spend five minutes MINIMUM a day filling this in, breathing into it. Observing the world around you and your life. We are creatures of habit and when we form a mindset that looks for the good, then we quickly duplicate that in a sense; like muscle memory. Repetition forms habit. If you start out struggling with finding the good, find something easy that isn't directly related to your experience. Such as, a blue sky, a summer's breeze, the stillness of a winter's night.

Appreciate the creation around us that has nothing to do with us, then work your way into, gratitude; for the way your child smiles after a meal, the way your dog's paws smell (don't judge me) or how much you love a chair on your deck or your favorite TV show. Then, as you get better at it, start to really look at your life and forget the stuff you may not be happy with, and think of all that you are happy with. Once you find one or two, they start to multiply. You are grateful for your car, you are grateful that you have a job that you are passionate about, you are grateful that you have a partner willing to stand by you, or you are grateful you are no longer with the partner holding you back.

That last one is important. Look at everything that has a negative and a positive angle and CHOOSE the positive angle. As I said, it's hard at first, but repetition becomes a habit. This is part of course-correcting your life and doubling down for happiness and your future. I can also tell you, becoming a more positive person is infectious. People will sense the change and often want to join in; but know sometimes the wrong people in your circle will try and attack this peace. That's where you have to do everything in your power to use the lessons of shifting mindset and positivity to fight off that bad juju and stay true to your new internal constitution.

You owe it to yourself to be happy. Life is so much shorter than we realize, and the opportunity to live our dreams shrinks every day we get closer to our death. So, ultimately, why not enjoy every day along the way or you'll end up on your deathbed regretting all the missed opportunities to be happy and find joy.

On top of overcoming depression and negativity this is how you allow yourself to up your threshold for pain when it comes to risk taking. I've talked all book about the importance of putting yourself out there, reaching back into your pocket to give more of yourself, having a willingness to get knocked down and get back up again . . . this is hard for mere mortals who forget about the joy that comes from small victories, and the happiness from knowing life happens for us and not to us.

This revelation leads to us to course-correcting ourselves . . . for the future. So now, you'll be more willing to take risks in life, love, business, etc. Interestingly enough, the concept of "course-correcting," as I'm talking about here, is in terms a more macro shift in your life. From another perspective there is a very important philosophy that must be embraced regarding a more micro sense of course-correction. This is the concept that frequently we need to be course-correcting in order to right our paths. We need to look at all aspects of our life in a fluid manner; constantly looking for opportunities for improvement, humility and shifting in order to get us on the path we need to be on.

I'd like to look at a large body of water as our metaphor for life in this example. Water truly is a blank canvas and often for a ship there are multiple destinations, islands, sandbars, rocks, waves and many obstacles along the way. When you fish, but you fish in one place for too long, you have to search for better waters; fish move, weather changes…it really is a perfect mirror to life. Throughout each day you have to make micro adjustments in order to keep you on your path and headed correctly on your journey.

The other element to this water metaphor is the fact that it is wide open, and you don't have to stay in a perfect line; you just have to stay on a set course. Also know that sometimes going off course takes you to where you are supposed to be, at that moment. Maybe staying on path would have led you into a school of sharks, or maybe choppy waves with no fish, or unexpected danger. Maybe the current will pull you to a beautiful island that you had no idea was there. I get it; it's a far-out analogy . . . but is it really?

I have gone fishing with my girlfriend's father a few times, and like any good fisherman who can call themselves a local to a certain area, they have their "spots," which they know tends to be a honey pot for catching. We now have the technology to save these locations on our boat GPS devices. So, you go back, you check out these areas every time, and I always find that interesting. We've got hundreds of miles in every direction but, somehow, we pick the same five spots to go to. As someone who didn't grow up fishing, I look around and wonder what else is out there…are there better spots?

This is such a perfect analogy of an entrepreneur; we are always wondering what else is out there. Course-correction is an invaluable skill for entrepreneurs. We have to have a spirit for adventure. Trying new things constantly, or otherwise you will get beaten up along the way and be miserable and confused why things aren't working out. WITH THAT SAID, entrepreneurs get bored a bit too easily, and although I am wondering what other fishing spots there might be out there, I also understand that on occasion I need to relax, drink a beer, have the line out there and just stick to what works and enjoy the breeze.

I have no idea how I went so far out there on the fishing and boat analogy, but it seemed like a great comparison, so I went with it.

Another great analogy when it comes to micro adjustments and corrections is during a baseball game. Every pitch is different based on the pitch prior. Many people are working with each other in order to orchestrate their best opportunity for victory. They replace batters, replace pitchers, replace runners. Based on the count with the batter they aim for a different spot, throw a different kind of pitch.

Baseball games have one major game plan that you start the game with. But just like most sports, it is used more as a guide than an exact straight-line path. Life is going to throw everything at you, and this micro course-correction is instrumental to your success. Same with keeping your chin up. Striking out or giving up a home run feels like crap at the time but remember in baseball there are twenty-seven outs on both sides. In life, on the other hand, there are a near infinite number of potential outcomes, if you just maintain the thought process that hard work, dedication and learning from mistakes pays off. Throughout that, have a good attitude and life will be fulfilling no matter what the score is.

Expand it ever more, baseball isn't just one game at any level. Baseball is a season, and that season is part of a career. You course-correct during a game, during a season, and ultimately each year you learn what to do differently to improve yourself for the next year. Sometimes you're going to lose, and in that you learn. When you win, learn to enjoy it, but don't let it linger. It's a balancing act. But when its simplicity is mastered, you have officially taught yourself how to override the system.

Also, everyone's gauge of fulfillment is different. It's important to find someone as a partner in life or in business who shares values in this sense. You don't have to be the same across the board, but your values are what are important. Another part of this balancing act is knowing you need to be with someone who strives for the same levels as you, but can embrace the positives and negatives that come along the way. This makes an unstoppable partnership, and often if someone is struggling, either in life or in business, this is the big shift that has to happen.

A "successful" business partner doesn't always make up for the culture and attitude it takes to have a business that is healthy and fulfilling. There are plenty of multi-millionaires who are miserable, and there are plenty of millionaires who fail in other business structures because of leadership dynamics. If this book resonates with you, find someone who can look at failure and success the same way you do. Find someone who can bounce back from failure and share your level of joy when things go right . . . or when you hit Blackjack, as I've said earlier.

Positive people always believe things happen for a reason, this is the ULTIMATE set up for success and happiness. That's how you have mental fortitude. Period. Hard stop.

Double Down or Bust

So now, how do double down from this point on and make a change in your life?

Make changes today. In the initial "note from the author," I talked about the difference between theorists and practitioners. At this point, I implore you to get your sh*t together and make the changes necessary in your life to make a shift in your perspective. We know at this point we have established that success and happiness have merged into one life path and one vision.

So, how do you double down on your mission to find happiness and success? The key to changing your life is to actually make changes. Embrace the hard, learn to feed off the trials and tribulations and make that a part of growth. This is why weightlifters and athletes push themselves to failure, because the more you challenge yourself, the stronger and more resilient you become.

One of the easiest things you can do to change your perspective is really quite simple. Exercise! Do something; get off your butt and exercise if you aren't already.

Invest in yourself, join networking and mastermind groups. You become the people you surround yourself with. You are looking to be happier, hang out with more positive and happy people. If you are looking to be more successful, in whatever your field is, surround yourself with successful people.

Sometimes doubling down on yourself includes leaving some things behind . . . and those things include material items and, yes, people.

And part of being a practitioner is TAKING ACTION. Tony Robbins calls this taking massive action. Don't wait until you are "ready." Take action now. When you put this book down make a list of what you are going to do, and then actually DO IT.

Now before anyone writes me, upset that they quit their job and didn't know where to go, when I say take massive action, that also means to calculate your steps. Set yourself up for success by working harder, grinding extra hours and putting yourself in a position to be ready to leave that job. Leave what is holding you back and learn from the mistakes you've made. Most importantly, don't sulk in them. This is when you take all of your mistakes and use them. Use them as fire for your soul, learn them as the lights along your path that teach you where to go.

This is when you take every hope, dream and wish you have wanted in your life and move towards it. Move towards it with reckless abandon and GET IT DONE. You deserve it. Anyone who wants it bad enough to make it all the way through this book wants it. Now it's just putting it all together and making it happen. Continue to read books, continue to take courses, continue to be inspired but don't forget to act on your desires. Take risks, some calculated, some just letting the wind take your sails. Live life without fear.

So with the memory of my father, and with all the positives, I want to lean into the negatives that made me who I am today. His gambling addiction lead me to the conclusion that in life there are no table limits. We can always keep doubling down. We can always reach back into our hearts and find another gear. Don't be afraid to go all-in for your dreams . . . you deserve happiness. Just remember deserving happiness isn't enough. You have to seek it with passion and with understanding that the easy road will never get you to the destination you dream of.

So fail, fail again, and remember failures are the stepping stones to success and happiness.

Acknowledgments

Thank you to those that were willing to throw caution to the wind and fail over and over in order to create this amazing world in which we now live. Despite its issues, our advancements would not be possible without those who were brave enough to fail, get up, and fail again.

On a more personal level I have to thank my partner in crime (and life), Kelly Allen, for kicking me in the shins until I finished this book, in what ended up being a three-year process.

Thank you to my mother, Phyllis, who has always been there to support me.

And lastly, my Dad. Lenny passed away in 2014, but it turns out his flaws were the ultimate fuel to my success. Like most people, he failed more than he succeeded, and it turns out that his gambling addiction paved the way for the creation of one of the greatest tools I would ever receive.

About the Author

nthony Russo has made it his life's work to master the art of motivation. As a child, Anthony was no stranger to difficult circumstances and struggles. Born into poverty and the son of a gambling addict Anthony realized that if he ever wanted to make something of himself, he would have to forge his path. Throughout his forty years, Anthony has dealt with countless struggles. From being diagnosed with hypoglycemia, bad ankles, and bad feet as a child; experiencing eviction; and coping with failures in business and relationships, Anthony managed to conquer his adversities.

Now, Anthony is a successful businessman who accomplished a seven-figure business within eighteen months with no start-up capital. He's also hosted major NCAA Championships and other large national events. Anthony has been featured in *Forbes* and *Inc Magazine,* where he talks about business and leadership. Furthermore, Anthony has worked with global brands like the Superbowl, Fox Big Noon Kickoff, tech conferences, country music TV and festivals, as well as major branded tours. He's also run eight marathons, and five half marathons; so much for those bad ankles.

Anthony's success has allowed him to dig deep within himself and connect to his purpose in life. He uses it as a driving force to continually progress forward and create a life that is vivid, diverse, and well-lived.

Today, Anthony is dedicated to helping others master motivation and personal power. Through the "#BeTheChange" movement, he harnesses his passion for individual responsibility to enable others to improve the world around them. Specifically, he teaches individuals how to bridge political divides, gain control of their lives, serve the less fortunate, and make small, impactful contributions to our broader communities.

Anthony also teaches a course, Double Down: *The Art of Negative Progression,* where he helps top executives, sales teams, and student leaders find their springboard of motivation and perseverance along with the playfulness required to enjoy the process.

A free ebook edition is available with the purchase of this book.

To claim your free ebook edition:

1. Visit MorganJamesBOGO.com
2. Sign your name CLEARLY in the space
3. Complete the form and submit a photo of the entire copyright page
4. You or your friend can download the ebook to your preferred device

Morgan James
BOGO™

A **FREE** ebook edition is available for you or a friend with the purchase of this print book.

CLEARLY SIGN YOUR NAME ABOVE

Instructions to claim your free ebook edition:
1. Visit MorganJamesBOGO.com
2. Sign your name CLEARLY in the space above
3. Complete the form and submit a photo of this entire page
4. You or your friend can download the ebook to your preferred device

Print & Digital Together Forever.

Snap a photo   Free ebook   Read anywhere